GARDENING IN THE CAROLINAS

Gardening in the
CAROLINAS

ARNOLD AND CONNIE

KROCHMAL

DOUBLEDAY & COMPANY, INC.
GARDEN CITY, NEW YORK
1975

Library of Congress Cataloging in Publication Data

Krochmal, Arnold, 1919–
    Gardening in the Carolinas.

    Bibliography: p. 229.
    Includes index.
        1. Gardening—North Carolina. 2. Gardening—South Carolina. 3. Plants,
Ornamental—North Carolina. 4. Plants, Ornamental—South Carolina. I.
Krochmal, Connie, joint author. II. Title.
SB453.2.N8K76   635.9′09756
ISBN 0-385-02529-7
Library of Congress Catalog Card Number 74–25112

The Talmud tells us there is no prescribed measure for deeds of kindness or study. The life of Dr. Lewis Knudson, formerly Chairman and Professor, Botany Department, Cornell University, was a living testimonial to these precepts. This book is dedicated to his memory because he thought as much of his students as he did of his research with plants, and contributed prodigiously to both.

Foreword

Some thirty-plus years ago when Arnold and I were students I recall his spending his summers working for the Horticulture Department at North Carolina State College, as it was known then, often on his knees pulling crab grass out of the departmental rose garden.

In the intervening years Arnold has never lost his enthusiasm and love of plants, and has finally, as I had expected, returned to make his permanent home in North Carolina.

In this book Arnold and his wife Connie present a useful series of tools for the garden enthusiast, whose efforts not only enhance the beauty of his home and community, but play a role in environmental protection and the maintenance of an improving ecology, rather than a degenerating ecology.

Descriptions of the adaptability of lawns, shrubs, trees, bulbs, annuals, and perennials for the three major areas of the Carolinas are presented in handy form, each with an introductory section. For the gardener who wants to propagate some of his own plants there is a detailed and well-illustrated chapter on propagating techniques.

Gardening is a major contribution to the economy of the Carolinas in terms of land use, hours employed, fertilizers and pesticides used, tools and equipment, and value of nursery plants, and rightfully so. In these days it is hard to find so much pleasure and healthful activity for so small an investment as a garden provides. The book Arnold and Connie have written will enhance the pleasure.

JAMES A. GRAHAM
Commissioner of Agriculture
North Carolina

Acknowledgments

We wish to acknowledge the help and cooperation given us by a number of friends. Our chapter on beach gardening depends heavily on the excellent publication "Seacoast Plants of the Carolinas," U. S. Department of Agriculture, Soil Conservation Service, written by Karl Graetz, retired Plant Materials Specialist.

Karl enthusiastically helped us locate illustrations we required. John Wiggins of Soil Conservation Service, U. S. Department of Agriculture, lent us needed photos.

Dr. C. Ritchie Bell, Professor of Botany, University of North Carolina, gave us some valuable comments on the structure of the book; Mary Cowell, Photo Librarian, U. S. Department of Agriculture, Washington, D.C., was most helpful locating illustrative materials; Dr. Jim Baker, Extension Entomologist, Department of Entomology, North Carolina State University, Raleigh, generously provided a chapter on insects and his own handsome hand-drawn insect sketches. Drs. Russ Southall, Galy Jividen, Henry J. Smith, and James Hardin of North Carolina State University read parts of the manuscript and made helpful suggestions.

Scott Lawns, Marysville, Ohio, provided useful information based on their many years of experience.

Mike Moose provided two handsome hand-drawn sketches of mobile-home landscapes, and enthusiastic encouragement.

Gardening has been called a lot of things. In large measure it is work, sweat, frustrations, and eventually a feeling of deep pleasure when a plant, shrub, or bulb bursts into bright and vivid bloom, or a tree grows with grace and strength.

We like all plants and enjoy them. We look with pleasure in the early spring at the cheerful yellow heads of daffodils that line our driveway, sometimes with the snow still lying on the ground.

When the Japanese aucuba we got from the North Carolina Botanical Garden clearly showed it would live and flourish on a steep slope behind our house we were as elated as parents of a new baby.

One spring we found ourselves bringing home all of the half-dead shrubs a nearby discount store would let us have at half price. We nursed and cajoled the shrubs to live, pruned, fertilized, and watered, and our pleasure at their survival is hard to write about. And we had saved quite a bit of money. For a while we hauled in all sorts of half-dead shrubs wherever we found the waifs, until we ran out of space. Now we can only look at other such plants wistfully in the nursery.

Gardening is as much an art, a thing of spirit and emotion, as it is a science. We have written this book as a contribution to the science. Our readers, we know, will provide in full measure the art.

A & CK
Asheville, N.C.

Contents

GARDENING IN THE CAROLINAS

1. Middleton Gardens, Charleston, S.C. (Photo courtesy
South Carolina Travel Bureau)

CHAPTER 1

Gardens and the Carolinas

From earliest colonial times gardens have been a major part of the life of the Carolinas, from the plantations to the centers of population.

A very deep love of plants has been a feature of life in both states and continues to this day. The first camellias in the New World were planted at Middleton Plantation in Charleston in the 1780s by André Michaux, a great French botanist.

To this day Middleton Plantation Gardens remains a well-worthwhile visitors' mecca (Figure 1). Considered America's oldest landscaped garden, it was carved in 1741 from wilderness by Henry Middleton, president of the First Continental Congress. The Plantation includes restorations of old buildings.

Charleston itself, in the Battery area, is rich in gardens differing little from those that were carefully cared for in the eighteenth century. Lovely old trees, quiet walks, and secluded yards are to be seen, some through the gates, others open to the public at specific times. Even the historic graveyards have handsome trees and shrubs.

Seventeen miles from Charleston is Boone Hall, a pre-Revolutionary plantation and a mansion with well-kept formal gardens featuring azaleas and camellias. There are nine of the original pre-Revolutionary servant cabins on view. A three-quarter-mile avenue of handsome patriarchal live oaks, covered with Spanish moss, is a sight of grandeur.

Quite different are the Cypress Gardens, twenty-three miles north of Charleston, operated in part by the City of Charleston. The most interesting sights here are the waterway and the lake with majestic bald cypresses and the ever present Spanish moss. Over three hundred varieties of camellias have been planted, as well as azaleas, wisteria, and many other horticultural delights.

The Charles Towne Landing, a state park outside Charleston, has 50 acres of handsome garden area. But we are most enchanted by the associated exhibits that take the visitor gracefully back in history to pre-colonial and colonial times. In one garden are planted crops once grown in the area but now only a memory. Here is a patch of indigo plants, once a major crop; next to it is a planting of tea, a flooded area with rice, figs, grapes, and pomegranates, and sea-island cotton.

Nearby is the 1,670-animal forest, 20 lovely acres of woods inhabited by the animals the early settlers saw and often ate. A museum, a replica of a trading ketch, and the restored settlement areas are all parts of this splendid garden.

Moving north to the Tarheel State, we find again a richness of gardens that is indeed a gourmet's delight.

In the western part of North Carolina there are at least two areas of unmatched beauty. One is the Great Smoky Mountains National Park. Wild plants in unbelievable profusion, from the high mountains to protected valleys, make this park a horticulturist's and gardener's paradise. Six hundred and fifty miles of nature trails take the visitor through the Canadian type of fir stands, above 6,000 feet elevation, to the flame azaleas which range from the 5,000 feet elevation down to the lowlands.

Close by are the famed Biltmore Gardens, outside of Asheville, 12,000 acres that one time were 100,000 acres bought by multimillionaire George Washington Vanderbilt.

The center of visiting gardeners' attraction is 17 acres of flowers with something blooming and growing every month of the year, and over five thousand roses in bloom from May to October. There is also a 35-acre formal garden featuring boxwoods, azaleas, English ivy, and wisteria in separate areas.

If you are driving east from Asheville and are near Kings

2. Pemberton Oak (Photo courtesy U. S. Forest Service)

Mountain Battlefield memorial, a trip to the Pemberton Oak (Figure 2) is a pilgrimage you may want to undertake. Here Colonel John Pemberton rallied his colonial militia for the Revolutionary battle of Kings Mountain, in 1781. This tree was a mature oak at that time, as the countrymen assembled with muskets to fight for hearth and home.

Unique in the Carolinas is the North Carolina Botanical Garden at Chapel Hill. The result of the vision and untiring efforts of Dr. C. Ritchie Bell, Professor of Botany at the University of North Carolina, the garden focuses on wild plants. A number of habitat groups are established for the visitor to see, including swamps.

Only wild, native plants are used. Short courses at the garden are scheduled, and a garden representative gives talks in the state to school groups.

North Carolina's first colonial capital, Tryon Palace, in New Bern is a worthwhile stop. Very formal (Figure 3), most of the garden is planted with shrubs, trees, and flowers available before 1770. There is an herb garden for kitchen use, and handsome evergreen plantings with graceful statues.

Farther on between Wilmington and Southport is Orton Plantation, once a colonial palace, the home of "King Roger" Moose, a showy, extravagant, and lavish extrovert. Extensive plantings of azaleas, wisteria, dogwood, and jasmine abound in the area, as well as acres of formal gardens (Figure 4).

In Wilmington, Greenfield Gardens is a glowing tribute to a city

3. Tryon Palace, New Bern, N.C. (Photo by Jim Page courtesy North Carolina Department of Natural and Economic Resources)

4. Orton Plantation, Wilmington, N.C. (Photo by Jim Page courtesy North Carolina Department of Natural and Economic Resources)

concerned enough about the aesthetics of urban living to do something tangible in its behalf. Greenfield is built around a scenic millpond, now a five-fingered lake covering 125 acres (Figure 5). Featured is a sunken garden of native flowers. The insectivorous Venus's-flytrap grows in the garden, as well as water lilies, jonquils, holly, hawthorn, and crab apples. Children's playgrounds, picnic sites, a theater, and fishing are available.

Unique indeed is the Elizabethan Garden, a project of the Garden Club of North Carolina, on famed Roanoke Island, site of Sir Walter Raleigh's lost colony.

5. Greenfield Gardens, Wilmington, N.C. (Photo by Jim Page courtesy of North Carolina Department of Natural and Economic Resources)

Combining local wild plants such as yaupon and dogwood with azaleas, magnolias, and a host of other aromatic and decorative plants, the garden is designed in the formal tradition of the Elizabethan era, a living memorial to the settlers of the lost colony who disappeared on the shores of the New World in 1587 (Figure 6).

Many other handsome gardens are on show in the Carolinas, but space does not allow us to discuss all. We have included a list, and state travel agencies can provide more detail.

6. Elizabethan Garden, Manteo, N.C. (Photo by Charles Clark courtesy of North Carolina Department of Natural and Economic Resources)

GARDENS OF NORTH CAROLINA

MOUNTAINS
    Biltmore Gardens, Asheville
    Daniel Boone Native Garden, Boone

PIEDMONT PLATEAU
    North Carolina Botanical Garden, Chapel Hill

COASTAL PLAINS
    Airlie Gardens, Wilmington

Bonner House Garden, Bath
Clarendon Gardens, Pinehurst
Elizabethan Garden, Manteo
Greenfield Gardens, Wilmington
Orton Plantation, Wilmington
Tryon Palace, New Bern

GARDENS OF SOUTH CAROLINA

PIEDMONT PLATEAU

Edisto Memorial Gardens, Orangeburg
Glencairn Garden, Rock Hill
Macey Gregg Rose Garden, Columbia
Rose Hill Historical Garden, Union
Swan Lake Gardens, Sumter
Boylston Gardens, Columbia

COASTAL PLAINS

Bell Isle Gardens, Georgetown
Bomar Gardens, Cheraw
Boone Hill Plantation, Charleston
Brookgreen Gardens, Murrells Inlet
Charles Towne Landing, Charleston
Cypress Gardens, Charleston
Kalmia Gardens, Hartsville
Magnolia Gardens, Charleston
Middleton Plantation Gardens, Charleston

CHAPTER 2

Climate

We have divided the Carolinas into three major regions (Figure 7) from west to east, differing in altitude, rainfall, temperature, and length of growing season. The regions are the Appalachian mountains, the Piedmont plateau, and the coastal plains. A subdivision of the coastal plains region is the seashore, which has some very special characteristics.

The gardener should remember that although the maps show the major regions clearly defined, no such sharp demarcation really exists. Conditions blend gradually from region to region, and pockets within a region may vary from the principal climatic factors in nearby areas.

Using the maps as a base, plus experience, the gardener can minimize climatic problems.

Last Freeze and First Freeze

Of prime importance in the setting out of annuals is the date of last freeze in the spring. We have used government data to plot lines (isotherms) (Figure 8) on the maps to show important gardening weather phenomena in the Carolinas.

If you examine Figure 9, Average date of the last freezing temperature (32°) in the spring, you can locate your own area on an isotherm, or interpolate between two isotherms to find the last frost date in your area.

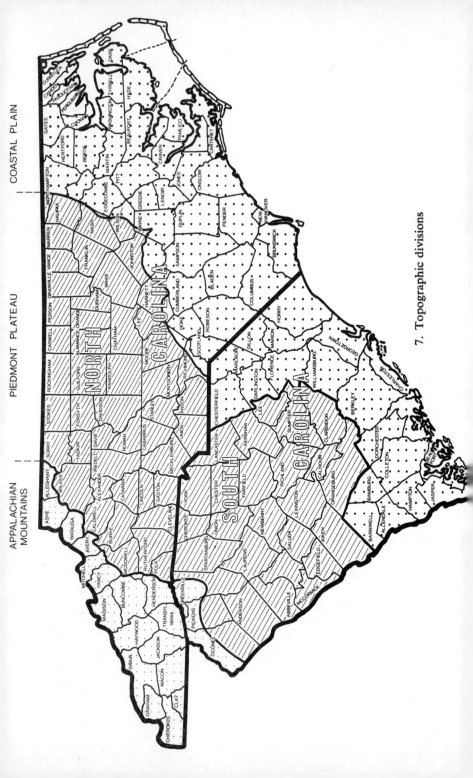

7. Topographic divisions

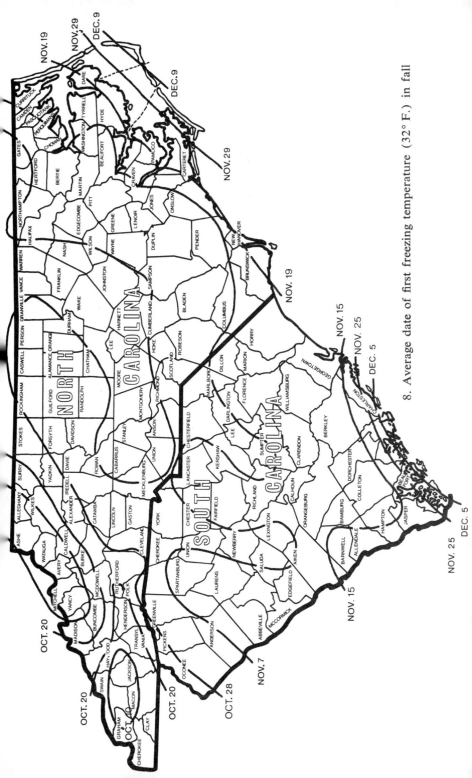

8. Average date of first freezing temperature (32° F.) in fall

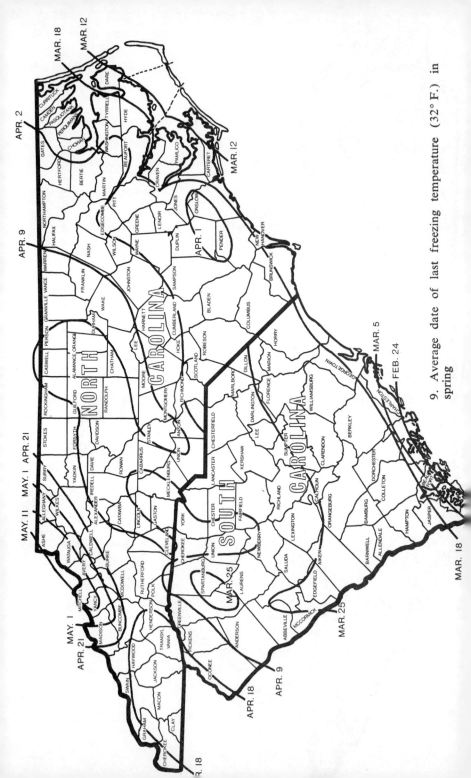

9. Average date of last freezing temperature (32° F.) in spring

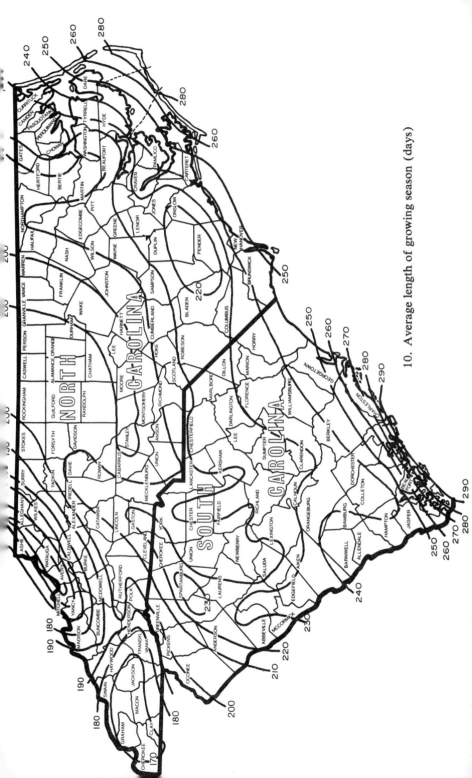

10. Average length of growing season (days)

The date arrived at is not fixed, but only an *average* date for a number of years. In the spring it is useful to be cautious and add a week or ten days to the average date of the last frost, to reduce damage risk to young and tender plants set out in the garden. Thus if average last frost in Raleigh is April 9, we would recommend setting out plants April 15.

In the fall preparation for winter can be based on the average date of first freezing temperature (Figure 8). We prefer to be cautious, and any shrubs we plan to protect from winter damage by wrapping or moving indoors we move a week or so before average first frost is expected. First frost in Raleigh averages October 28. Wrapping and moving indoors can begin October 15.

The length of the growing season (Figure 10) represents the average number of days between the average date of last frost and the average date of first frost. This information can be helpful in planning a schedule for continuous blooming as well as aiding in selecting shrubs that will do their best with the growing season in your region.

Water

In areas where water may be somewhat scarce, or expensive, knowledge of the average annual rainfall (Figure 11) will help you select plants most suited for the rainfall and available supplemental water. With rising water rates, it can also help determine approximately how much supplemental water will be needed, and the cost.

Preparing for Winter

Some gardeners wrap valuable shrubs as protection against extremely low temperature during winter. Materials that can be used include burlap, plastic, and even cornstalks. Any of these can be wrapped and tied around the plant. We have always left one branch of evergreens exposed. There is no solid foundation in science for leaving a branch unwrapped, other than the "feeling" that even a little photosynthesis activity producing plant food is better than none at all. Wrapping should be removed in the spring when frost danger is over.

If shrubs, perennials, and trees have been chosen with the help of the temperature charts in this chapter the plants should be

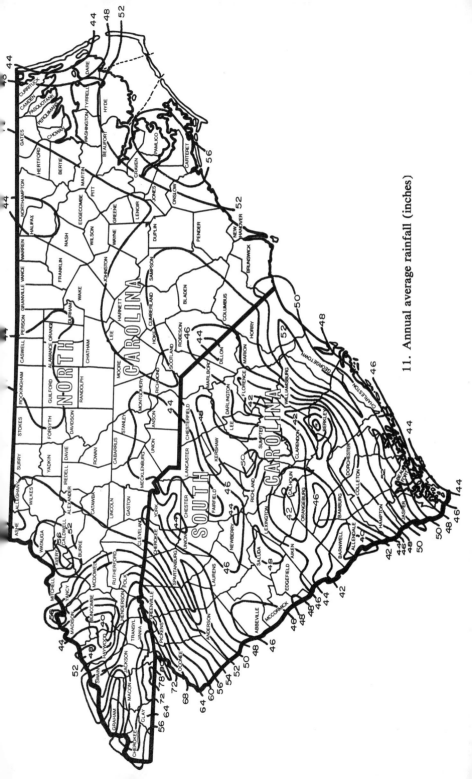

11. Annual average rainfall (inches)

reasonably well adapted to the climate of the area. There are also some long-range as well as immediate programs to minimize frost danger.

Healthy and well-nourished disease-free trees will better withstand low temperature than diseased trees in a poor state of health. *However,* if nitrogen fertilizers are added late in the summer, green, tender growth will result. Such growth is particularly sensitive to freeze damage.

If your land slopes, remember that cold air settles into low spots, and it is advisable to plant hardier plants in such low spots.

Low Temperature and Ice Damage

If, despite all efforts, trees and shrubs are damaged by freezes or ice accumulation, there are measures the gardener can take to remedy the damage.

Firstly, some idea must be formulated as to the severity of the damage. If the tree or shrub seems beyond repair, it may be well to replace it. However, if it seems to have possibilities of survival, steps can be taken to save the plant.

If a limb is badly torn or broken, cut it back to the nearest sound limb, or the trunk of the plant. Tree paint available at garden shops and nurseries can be applied to the cut surface to reduce chances of insect or disease invasion.

If a tree or shrub is partially heaved out of the ground there are possibilities of getting it back to a near-normal state. However, it is a hard job and failures will probably equal successes.

The top should be pruned to balance with the destroyed roots. At the same time the shape of the plant must be maintained as well as possible. Clear the soil from the exposed heaved roots to make replacement in the hole as damage-free as possible. Drive in three strong stakes about 3 to 5 feet from the outer perimeter of the lower branches, at an angle, leaning away from the trunk.

We have used plastic clothesline to keep a damaged tree erect. A wide range of materials can be used. However, if a tree is fairly large the material should be one that will not stretch. A heavy nylon rope will do well. We fasten rope about halfway up the trunk, being careful not to damage limbs and branches.

For this sort of operation at least two people are needed. If the plant is bulky three people are somewhat more reassuring.

Flooding

During an "unexpected" spring flood at the lower end of our property in Raleigh part of our land was under a foot of water for several hours. We noted no damage to the trees or to the wild plant population adjacent to our land. However, we would dread a repetition.

RECOMMENDED REFERENCES

Department of Commerce of North Carolina, *Climatological Data.* Vol. 75, No. 6, Raleigh, N.C. 27607, June 1970.

North Carolina Agricultural Extension Service, *Climate of North Carolina Research Stations.* Bulletin 433, North Carolina State University, Raleigh, N.C. 27607, July 1967.

————, *Protecting Plants from Cold Damage.* Horticultural Information Leaflet No. 500, North Carolina State University, Raleigh, N.C. 27607, October 1965.

————, *Repair to Ice-Damaged Trees and Shrubs.* Horticultural Information Leaflet No. 518, North Carolina State University, Raleigh, N.C. 27607, January 1968.

————, *Weather and Climate in North Carolina.* Bulletin 396, North Carolina State University, Raleigh, N.C. 27607, October 1971.

South Carolina Agricultural Extension Service, *Length of the Growing Season in South Carolina.* Agricultural Weather Research Series No. 13, Clemson University, Clemson, S.C. 29631, March 1967.

U. S. Department of Commerce, *Climate of the States—Climates of South Carolina.* Climatography of the United States NO60-38, Washington, D.C. 20250, June 1970.

12. A sample screened-in compost heap (Photo courtesy
U. S. Department of Agriculture)

CHAPTER 3

Soils and Their Care

Soil Testing

The kinds of soils used for gardens will vary tremendously. Sometimes a builder scrapes the topsoil away; another new home may have all sorts of plaster and trash dumped over parts of the garden. An older home may have the garden area in good condition.

Bringing soil into productivity and maintaining it requires physical as well as chemical treatment.

A first step is to have the soil analyzed, a service available in both Carolinas at state-operated soil-testing laboratories. These laboratories not only analyze the soil but also recommend fertilizers to be used for whatever purpose is under consideration, from lawns to flower beds.

South Carolinians should mail their soil sample to:

Agronomy Department
Clemson University
Clemson, S.C.   29631

North Carolinians can send their samples to:

Soil Testing Division
North Carolina Department of Agriculture
Raleigh, N.C.   27611

Fertilizers

The garden requires a proper balance of soil minerals for plant growth. The gardener will generally concern himself with nitrogen (N), phosphorus (P), and potassium (K). Other nutrients play a role but are less likely to be deficient.

Fertilizers contain the three main elements needed for plant growth; nitrogen, phosphorus, and potassium. The percentage of each can be found on the bag. A 5–5–5 formula means that fertilizer contains 5 per cent of total nitrogen, 5 per cent of available phosphoric acid, and 5 per cent of soluble potash.

The larger the total of these three numbers, the more expensive the fertilizer, because you pay for the mineral ingredients. Thus a 5–10–5 has a total of 20 units, and a 6–12–6 has 24 units.

The ratio of the primary nutrients in a fertilizer relates to the adaptability of the fertilizer for specific plants and soils. Fertilizers for lawns are high in nitrogen, essential for vegetative growth, but fertilizer for flowering plants may have high proportions of phosphoric acid, important for flowering.

Fertilizers for special plant use are available, such as rose fertilizer, azalea fertilizer, lawn fertilizers, and such. However, they are more expensive than ordinary farm or garden fertilizers.

Fertilizers having the same proportion of N-P-K can be used interchangeably—a 5–10–5 would be used in one half the amount of a 10–20–10.

In buying fertilizer it often pays to buy the mix with the highest analysis. A 40-unit bag may be cheaper in cost of *actual fertilizer* than a 24-unit mix. The quantity of N, P, or K desired for any given area can be applied. The procedure is to apply a proportionately smaller amount of the higher-analysis fertilizer.

NITROGEN

Nitrogen is the costliest of the components of a bag of fertilizer and comes in two general forms—slowly available and quickly available. Slowly available forms such as urea and other organic forms become available over a longer period of time and cost more. Other forms of nitrogen are available more quickly. The major difference is that more than one application of the quicker forms may be needed.

Compost

Compost piles have been known and used for quite a while despite the impression one can gain that this is a new discovery. Compost is a priceless ingredient in improving garden soil, at modest cost. Mixed into the soil, a well-decayed compost loosens the soil, permitting freer air and soil water movement, and improves water-holding capacity.

The most practical compost pile will be made up of autumn leaves, lawn clippings, and other plant materials which will decay readily. Larger and heavier materials can be included after going through a mechanical shredder. Evergreens are too slow to decay; vegetable leftovers are all right but may smell and draw flies.

A sample screened-in area (Figure 12) using heavy chicken wire will be of help in keeping the compost in one area. The pile should be turned over with a spade because the older materials at the bottom will rot first.

The addition of fertilizer will hasten the breakdown of organic matter. As the new leaves (or other material) are laid down pack them to a depth of 6 inches, and then soak thoroughly. Then a cup of 5–10–5 or 6–12–6 (or as close to those formulas as you have available) is sprinkled for each 10 square feet. A cup of ground limestone is added in the same way. The same process is repeated as additional layers of plant materials are added.

Composting takes a year or two, longer at higher, cooler elevations, less in the lower areas. A compost laid down in the fall should be turned over in the spring (Figure 13) and again in midsummer. During dry spells wet the heap down.

Sometimes instead of a compost pile the leaves can be turned under in place if the area is used for annuals, or if a new area is to be planted the following spring (Figure 14).

Mulches

Mulches serve several purposes in soil and garden management. They conserve soil moisture and minimize weed growth. Under certain conditions mulches protect the soil from extremely high temperatures and from low winter temperatures. Over a period of time they add organic matter to the soil and help keep it in good physical condition.

The range of materials used is almost limitless. Sheets of black

13. Turning over a compost heap (Photo courtesy U. S. Department of Agriculture)

polyethylene laid on the surface of the ground are fine. If the plastic seems to present a discordant note in the garden, cover it with a layer of pine bark, soil, or pine needles.

Pine bark for mulch is readily available in nurseries and similar outlets. It is excellent, and we use several bales each year, applying it in the very early spring and early fall. We use a circle slightly smaller than the outer diameter of the shrubs, and 2 to 3 inches thick. We do not use mulches on older trees, but do for several years after we plant a young tree, whether evergreen or deciduous, and always around shrubs.

Pine needles can be used around older trees and seem to be well suited for use around azaleas and camellias. Other materials that are used for mulching include gravel, pine straw, peanut hulls, sawdust, aluminum foil, leaves, and peat moss.

14. Turning leaves into the soil of a planting site (U. S. Department of Agriculture photograph by Knell)

There is a belief that mulches will tend to change the soil pH, particularly when pine needles or pine straw are used. Any such change would be so slow as to be of no importance.

Sawdust as a mulch sometimes seems to stunt growth. The principal reason for this is the temporary tying-up of soil nitrogen, the result of the increased activity and larger numbers of soil bacteria and soil fungi which attack the sawdust, a source of energy. These microorganisms require nitrogen, which they get from the soil, tying it up until the decay of the sawdust is complete. The best way, then, to handle the problem is by adding nitrogen fertilizer when sawdust is used.

The nitrogen deficiency problem can occur with other plant materials turned under, but usually to a lesser degree. A smaller rate of application of nitrogen is recommended.

Working the Soil

It is sometimes a problem to know when the soil is right for working—not too wet. In Arizona a common belief is that if you shape a pig's head of soil but the ears won't stand up, the soil is too dry. The feel of the soil when it is right for working is something gained by experience. If a few handfuls of soil break up into large hunks, the soil is about right.

RECOMMENDED REFERENCES

Department of Conservation and Development of North Carolina, *Geology and Mineral Resources of North Carolina.* Education Series No. 3, Raleigh, N.C. 27607, 1953.

Minnesota Agricultural Extension Service, *Building a Compost Heap.* Fact Sheet Soils No. 12, University of Minnesota, St. Paul, Minnesota 55101.

North Carolina Agricultural Extension Service, *Conversion Tables.* Horticultural Information Leaflet No. 501. North Carolina State University, Raleigh, N.C. 27607, October 1965.

————, *Conversion Tables.* Horticultural Information Leaflet No. 417, North Carolina State University, Raleigh, N.C. 27607, August 1967.

————, *The Soils of North Carolina; Their Formation, Identification and Use.* Technical Bulletin 115, North Carolina State University, Raleigh, N.C. 27607, December 1965.

U. S. Department of Agriculture, *Selecting Fertilizer for Lawns and Gardens.* Home and Garden Bulletin No. 89, Washington, D.C. 20250, June 1971.

————, *The Use of Sawdust for Mulches and Soil Improvement.* Circular No. 891, Washington, D.C. 20250, November 1958.

CHAPTER 4

Lawns

A healthy, weed-free, bright green lawn is the keystone for the development of an interesting and pleasing garden program.

To achieve a desirable lawn requires the best possible soil site, the selection of the adapted grass or grasses to be planted at the desired time of the year, and the proper maintenance of the lawn based on optimum fertility, water supply, mowing, and control of weeds, diseases, and sod insects.

Establishment

If you buy a home already built, this phase is not your problem. If you are building a home, you can exercise some control over the construction program that will be of major importance in planning the best possible site for the future lawn.

(*1*.) The richer topsoil, up to 6 inches in depth, should be removed and piled on an area away from the construction site, for replacement later.

(*2*.) All trash and rubbish should be removed from the site.

(*3*). Keep in mind that maintenance of the lawn as you plan it, and remember, even power mowers require labor. Too steep slopes tend to wash, and terraces are expensive to install and maintain.

(*4.*) Poor drainage may call for tile drains. The average homeowner would do well to get skilled assistance for this job. Poor drainage can be judged after a rainfall. If surface water stands very long, or the soil remains wet for long periods of time, a drainage problem exists.

(*5.*) Concern for ecology is translated by progressive developers into an effort to leave as many trees as possible in place. If you find that a proposed new lawn will be much higher than the original soil level, existing trees may require protection. A simple way to do this is to build a wall of stone, brick, or concrete around the tree trunk, from the original level to where the new level will be. The wall should be from 1½ to 2½ feet out from the tree trunk, depending on how big the tree will grow ultimately.

At the outer base of the wall a layer of crushed gravel should be spread 8 to 10 feet outward. The new lawn level is built up to the height of the wall, all of which provides aeration for the tree.

SOIL AND SITE PREPARATION

The subsoil should be worked to a depth of 6 to 12 inches, depending on the soil type, lighter sandy soils 6 inches, heavier clay soils deeper. A spade or shovel can be used, or a roto-tiller or tractor and disk. Machinery saves human energy but costs more, of course.

If possible, the slope of the soil should be away from the house to reduce dampness problems. A slope of 2 per cent, 2 feet for every 100 feet, will usually give satisfactory surface drainage.

The topsoil that was set aside originally should now be spread evenly over the lawn area; a rake should be used to level the area. If the topsoil is sparse, more may be bought. If desired, peat moss, rotted leaves, or well-rotted manure can be added to the soil, at a rate of 1 to 2 cubic yards for each 500 square feet of lawn.

The soil may need lime and phosphate fertilizer. The soil-testing laboratories of the state Departments of Agriculture in Columbia and Raleigh will provide instructions for soil sampling as well as analysis to help determine correct amounts of fertilizers.

Pre-planting

After the lawn is level, and graded to your requirements, a spading or plowing, followed by a light disking or roto-tilling, and hand raking, are recommended to ready the site for planting.

The next step is the application of a complete fertilizer.

A broad lawn fertilizer recommendation, for soil that has not been analyzed, would be to broadcast for each 1,000 square feet of lawn 50 to 75 pounds of agricultural lime and a high nitrogen fertilizer, sometimes sold as lawn fertilizer, at the rate of 20 to 30 pounds. These special lawn fertilizers have nitrogen per cents *much higher* than the P and K per cents.

Seeding

The cost of the seed is the smallest part of the cost of a lawn. Select a grass adapted to your region and to the particular growing area, such as light shaded area, direct sun, good drainage, and so on. Seed with a high germination percentage and high purity is well worth a premium price.

Seed may be sown with a small mechanical seeder or by hand from a bucket. To help get uniform seeding sow first in one direction, and then again at right angles. When seeding is complete, rake the area to cover the seed about ¼ inch deep. Then add a pine needle or straw mulch at the rate of 1 bale to 1,000 square feet of lawn, to shade the young grass and protect it from drying. Light watering twice a day for fifteen minutes is recommended until the young grass appears, followed by watering once a day for fifteen to twenty minutes, working to watering at approximately weekly intervals.

Late August and September are considered the best time to renovate cool-season lawns, although bare areas or new lawns may be seeded in early spring. Lawn grasses make their best growth in the fall or spring.

Spring is the best time to plant warm-season grasses which grow best in the summer months.

Vegetative Planting

Some grasses are propagated by vegetative methods because seeds are scarce or not available, or do not produce true-to-type plants (Table 1). These methods are more expensive than seed, but an attractive lawn can be established much quicker this way. The different methods used are described below.

TABLE 1 THE PRINCIPAL GRASS VARIETIES AND THEIR CHARACTERISTICS FOR THE CAROLINAS

GRASS	TOPOGRAPHIC AREA	RATE OF SEEDING per 1,000 sq. ft.	SEASON	EXPOSURE	PLANTING TIME	COMMENTS
Bermuda (Cynodon dactylon)	all regions	2-3 lb. seed 10 sq. ft. sod[1] 1 bushel of stolons	warm	sun	spring-early summer	Turns brown in the fall. Widely used on beach areas, particularly "coastal" bermuda. It is salt-resistant, survives sand burial and flooding. Requires lots of fertilizer.
Centipede (Eremochloa ophiuroides)	coastal plains	8-10 sq. ft. sod[1] 2-3 lb. seed	warm	light shade to sun	spring-early summer	Resists weeds; low maintenance requirement; low water and fertilizer needs. Widely used on Carolina beaches. Soil pH should be no more than 5.8.
Ky. bluegrass (Poa pratensis)	Appalachian mts.; Piedmont plateau	1-2 lb. seed	cool	intolerant to heavy shade	fall	Requires liming on acid soils; drought-resistant.

[1]This amount is used for plugging with ¾" thick plugs set 1' apart.

GRASS	TOPOGRAPHIC AREA	RATE OF SEEDING per 1,000 sq. ft.	SEASON	EXPOSURE	PLANTING TIME	COMMENTS
Italian	all regions	3-4 lb. seed	cool	shade to sun	fall, sometimes early spring	In mixes Italian ryegrass may compete with Ky. bluegrass and fescue, excellent on slopes for erosion control.
Pensacola grass or bahia grass (*Paspalum notatum*)	coastal plains	1-1½ lb. seed	warm	sun	spring	Requires little maintenance and is considered disease-resistant. Excellent salt spray tolerance.
St. Augustine or Charleston grass (*Stenotaphrum secundatum*)	coastal plains	8-10 sq. ft. sprigs	warm	shade tolerant	spring	Withstands salt spray. Recommended for Charleston area; can be grown north to Atlantic Beach, N.C. Salt-resistant.
tall fescue (*Festuca arundinacea*)	Appalachian mts.; Piedmont plateau; coastal plains	5-6 lb. seed	cool	light shade to sun	fall	Resistant to insects and diseases; seeded with Ky. bluegrass; may brown in summer.

[1] This amount is used for plugging with ¾" thick plugs set 1' apart.

GRASS	TOPOGRAPHIC AREA	RATE OF SEEDING per 1,000 sq. ft.	SEASON	EXPOSURE	PLANTING TIME	COMMENTS
Zoysia (*Zoysia matrella*)	coastal plains; Piedmont plateau; lower elevations or Appalachian mts.	8-10 sq. ft. sprigs[1] or plugs	warm	light shade to full sun	spring-summer	Turns brown in the fall, takes up to three years to establish, resists drought, weeds, and salt spray.

[1] This amount is used for plugging with ¾″ thick plugs set 1′ apart.

(*1.*) *Sprigging* is the planting of individual plants or parts of plants at intervals in prepared holes. Sprigs are obtained by tearing apart established sod of the desired material. The planting distance is dictated by amount of propagating material available, as well as by rate of growth. Zoysia takes longer to fill in than Bermuda grass.

(*2.*) *Plugging* refers to using plugs of sod which grow slowly. Spacing principles are as above.

(*3.*) *Stolonizing* is a method requiring large quantities of stolons, or underground roots, which are cut up small and then planted, covered with soil, and tamped. Rapid coverage of Bermuda grass and zoysia grass would require as much as 5–10 bushels of stolons per 1,000 square feet.

(*4.*) *Sodding* is the most expensive method and is rarely used. Here whole strips of sod are transferred to a lawn site for "instant lawns." All of these methods have one thing in common and that is that the vegetative material must be kept moist until planted and then sprinkled regularly.

RECOMMENDED REFERENCES

Department of Pathology, *Controlling Lawn Grass Diseases*. Plant Pathology Information Note 182, North Carolina State University, Raleigh, N.C. 27607, June 1972.

North Carolina Agricultural Extension Service, *Carolina Lawns*. Extension Circular 292, North Carolina State University, Raleigh, N.C. 27607, March 1971.

U. S. Department of Agriculture, *Better Lawns*. Home and Garden Bulletin No. 51, Washington, D.C. 20250, July 1971.

———, *Lawn Diseases; How to Control Them*. Home and Garden Bulletin No. 61, Washington, D.C. 20250, August 1971.

———, *Lawn Insects; How to Control Them*. Home and Garden Bulletin No. 53, Washington, D.C. 20250, August 1971.

———, *Suggestions for Fall Lawn Care*. CA-34-14, Washington, D.C. 20250.

CHAPTER 5

Trees

There is difficulty at times in distinguishing a tree from a shrub, a distinction of not too much concern, except for mature plant size. For our purposes, a tree can be considered a woody plant with a single trunk, growing at maturity to over a height of 15 to 20 feet.

As we write this we look out our window and see bearing plum and peach trees 15 feet in height, which are definitely trees, and a bearing fig 10 feet tall, undoubtedly a shrub, although under optimum conditions figs can grow to 25 feet in height, or more.

USES

Trees are sources of shade, they may serve as sound and wind barriers, provide screening and privacy, offer refuge to a variety of birds and squirrels, and cut off unpleasant or uninteresting views. They are also, we find, comforting to have around.

In our yard we have the dignity of oak and the aroma of pine. Each year we see the beginning of life in the spring as buds swell, the development of flowers and heavy summer foliage, the onset of glowing fall colors, the loss of leaves, and dormancy. Sleeping in the cold weather, life goes on, and we know the cycle will repeat itself. When one of our trees dies, we use the wood in our fireplace, and looking into the warm flames recall the years the tree took to grow and reach old age, serving man all along the road of its life.

SELECTION

A tree bought from a local nursery will undoubtedly be adapted to your local environment. The major concern should be the adaptability of the tree at maturity to the purpose you intend it to serve. If you want to line a driveway, tall, slender trees will be much more suitable than broad, spreading trees. However, a spreading tree would be fine to provide shade for a patio or barbecue area. For one-story homes a tree growing to a maximum height of 30 to 40 feet is recommended. Too tall trees near a low-built home tend to dwarf the home.

TIME

Some trees are best planted in the spring to allow them ample time to become established.

Among these are dogwood, tulip poplar, magnolia, birch, hemlock, oak, and sassafras.

PLANTING AND CARE

The larger a tree the greater is the shock of transplanting to a new site. A small tree transplanted may well outgrow a large tree transplanted, over a period of years.

Much of the transplanting information in the shrub chapter applies to trees as well. Figure 15 summarizes methods of transplanting a tree with a ball of earth.

When a young tree is in position it is a wise precaution, after the soil has been packed around the roots, to provide the tree with support. For trees 3 inches or less in diameter use one or two metal fence posts sunk into soil next to the ball of earth. First wrap the trunk with strips of burlap, tying the burlap in place with heavy twine, then fasten the trunk to the fence posts with wire loops covered with sections of old garden hose (Figure 16).

Fertilizer

If you decide to fertilize a tree, measure the diameter of the tree at breast height (DBH), usually 4½ feet above ground level. For each inch of tree diameter at DBH, use 2 pounds of 5–10–5 or 6–12–6. Punch a series of holes 18 inches apart and 18 inches deep around the drip line of the tree (the diameter of the leafy part of the

  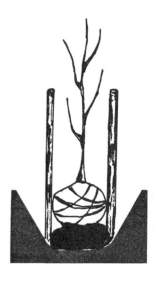

15. Left to right:
The planting hole should be large enough to hold the roots and a rich mixture of soil.
The planting hole is then filled until the soil surface is level with the top of the ball of earth.
Two supporting stakes are then driven into the soil on opposite sides of the ball of earth. (Courtesy U. S. Department of Agriculture)

tree), with no hole within a foot of the tree, and divide the fertilizer evenly among these holes. Then fill the holes with a soil and peat moss mixture.

RECOMMENDED TREES

Acer platanoides, Norway maple

Found in the Appalachian mountains, the Norway maple grows to 40 feet in height, and is a good shade tree. It is a rapid grower. Because the feeding roots are close to the surface, almost nothing will grow underneath the tree. The leaves turn yellow in autumn.

Acer rubrum, red maple, swamp maple, soft maple

This maple grows in all regions, and may reach a height of 70 feet. It is a rapid-growing shade tree, and does well in swampy areas, and preferably in rich soil. With red flowers appearing very early in the spring, the foliage usually turns a vivid red in the autumn, touched with yellow.

 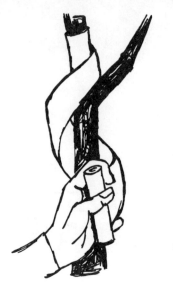 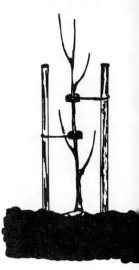

16. Left to right:
The soil is packed down and firmed, with whatever tools are useful. A ridge of soil is then thrown up to form a shallow basin to hold water near the tree. Then wrap the trunk with burlap strips, which can be cut from old burlap sacks. Tie the strips every 12 inches or so with strong cord. To help the tree grow straight it is then attached to the two supporting stakes with hose-covered wire, and watered well. (Courtesy U. S. Department of Agriculture)

Acer saccharum, sugar maple

The sugar maple grows in all regions to a height of 35 feet, and is well adapted to the Appalachians. It does best in moist areas in a rich soil, but will grow on poor soils as well. In autumn the leaves provide a spectacular show of color.

Amelanchier canadensis, serviceberry, shadbush

A small tree adapted to the Appalachian mountains, growing to a height of 35 feet. The small white flowers which bloom in masses in the spring last only a few days, and are followed by attractive red to purple fruits.

Betula nigra, river birch, red birch

The river or red birch grows in all regions to 30 to 50 feet in height, but is not too well adapted to the higher altitudes. It is rather short-lived and very difficult to transplant. Spring pruning is suggested. It does well in moist, sandy soils.

Carya spp., hickory

Hickory grows in all regions. It does best in moist locations. Buy trees from nurseries, because it is hard to transplant. Different species do well in different locations. *C. glabra* is suggested for all regions. *C. illinoensis* grows in the Piedmont and the coastal plain, from 35 to 70 feet in height. It does best in rich, moist bottomland.

Catalpa spp., catalpa

Catalpa grows in all regions. Eastern catalpa (*C. bignonioides*) is the most widely recommended variety. Water catalpa (*C. speciosa*) does well in hot summers and dry soil but grows to be much larger than practical. Both have showy white flowers developing into brown pods. They can accept neglect.

Celtis occidentalis, hackberry

This handsome tree or large shrub grows in all regions to a height of 30 to 40 feet. The small green flowers are followed by dark purple berries which remain on the tree into winter. It is drought-resistant, and will grow on rocky soils as well as good soils.

Cercis canadensis, eastern redbud, Judas tree (Figure 17)

This tree grows in all regions to a height of 35 feet. It blooms the same time as the flowering dogwood with the leaves appearing soon afterward. It does well in a sandy, fertile loam, in shade as well as sunlight. The bright red berries are as attractive as the handsome rose-colored flowers.

Chamaecyparis pisifera, sawara false cypress, Japanese sawara

This evergreen grows in the Piedmont and the coastal plain to a height of 50 feet in sun or partial shade on dry soils. It may have its foliage turn brown during the winter, and could be considered undesirable for this reason. It is related to cedars.

Cornus florida, flowering dogwood (Figure 18)

The flowering dogwood grows in all regions to a height of 25 feet. There are pink, white, and double-flowered forms as well as a weep-

17. *Cercis canadensis,* redbud (Photo courtesy U. S. Forest Service)

18. *Cornus florida,* dogwood (Photo courtesy U. S. Forest Service)

ing form, which produces bright red berries. It grows in a variety
of soils; it does best in a fertile loam with good drainage and
moderate moisture, but will do well in dry areas. Shade is desirable.
It is well suited for small properties, and is easily propagated from
seed collected in the fall and planted immediately. The seedlings do
best in partial shade.

Fagus grandifolia, American beech
   This beech does well in all regions. It is a magnificent specimen
tree with a bronze foliage color in the fall. The fibrous roots are
surface feeders, so the area below is usually bare of other plants, but
little beech trees will arise, and should be cut out.

Fraxinus americana, white ash
   White ash grows in all regions and may reach a height of 70 feet.
It does well in a variety of locations, but prefers a moist one. It
reproduces easily from seed, and adapts to partial shade or sun.
A rapid grower, it is not recommended for small properties.

Ginkgo biloba, ginkgo, maidenhair tree (Figure 19)
   The ginkgo grows in all regions. It is a slow grower that may
reach a height of 35 to 50 feet. The fruit grows only on female
trees, which are rarely planted. It is not a good tree for small
properties but is recommended as a specimen tree for a large lawn.
It does well in sun and survives high levels of pollution in urban
areas.

Gleditsia triacanthos, honeylocust, sweetlocust
   This tree grows in all regions to a height of 50 feet; it will grow in
various light and temperature conditions and is highly drought-resistant. The thornless horticultural variety is recommended since
the thorns dropping on the ground may be a safety hazard. It likes
rich, moist soils.

Ilex latifolia, lusterleaf holly
   This holly tree grows in the coastal plain to a height of 60 feet
and requires an acid soil and a shady location.

Ilex opaca, American holly (Figure 20)
   The American holly grows in all regions to 45 feet in height; it

19. *Ginkgo biloba,* ginkgo (Photo by Arnold Krochmal)

prefers part shade, but will do fairly well in full sun in a good, well-drained soil. Buying plants 2–4 feet tall is recommended as it may be possible at that size to tell whether it will bear berries (female) or not (male). If desired, cuttings may be taken in July or August from a female tree for propagation in a prepared bed.

Ilex verticillata, winterberry
Winterberry grows in the Appalachian mountains to a height of 30 feet, and has the same growth requirements as *I. opaca.*

Ilex vomitoria, yaupon (Figure 21)
The yaupon grows in the Piedmont and the coastal plain to a height of 15 feet. A slow grower, it is relatively drought-resistant and prefers an acid soil. It is propagated from cuttings usually taken from the female berry-bearing trees. It does not transplant easily from the wild. It adjusts to sun or shade, and is used along the seashore because it is resistant to salt spray.

20. *Ilex opaca,* American holly (Photo courtesy U. S. Forest Service)

Juglans spp., walnut (*J. nigra*), butternut (*J. cinerea*)
Both of these trees grow in all regions, and do well in rich, moist places. The long tap root makes it difficult to transplant. Walnut is better suited for planting than the butternut.

Juniperus virginiana, eastern red cedar, red cedar, savin
This tree grows in the coastal plain and the Piedmont to a height of 30 feet. It is well adapted to rocky soils. The needles when crushed are highly aromatic and the blue fruit is pea-sized and berry-like. It is a slow grower.

Lagerstroemia indica, crape myrtle
Crape myrtle grows in the Piedmont and the coastal plain to 20 feet in height. It grows best in the sun or partial shade, and propagates easily from cuttings. It should be pruned back drastically the first few years.

Liquidambar styraciflua, sweetgum
Difficult to transplant, sweetgum grows in all regions. It does best

21. *Ilex vomitoria,* yaupon (Photo courtesy U. S. Forest Service)

in moist locations, growing to 50 feet in height. Its attractive pyramidal shape and brilliant fall color make it a favorite specimen.

Liriodendron tulipifera, tuliptree, tulip poplar

This tree grows in all regions to a height of 30–50 feet. The yellow flowers are tulip-shaped, and the cucumber-like fruits can be messy on a lawn. It is relatively insect- and disease-free. Though it is not easily transplanted, it is a rapid grower. It does best in a moist, fertile soil.

Magnolia grandiflora, southern magnolia

Southern magnolia grows in all areas but is more common in the Piedmont and coastal plain. It grows to 35 feet in height, its flowers are 8 inches long, and the evergreen foliage is dark, glossy green. It prefers lots of room to grow, a moist soil, and sun or partial shade.

Magnolia virginiana, sweet bay, laurel magnolia

The sweet bay or laurel magnolia grows in the Piedmont and the coastal plain to 60 feet in height. Difficult to transplant, it is noted for its large, conspicuous white spring flowers and its large evergreen leaves. It can be grown in wet to swampy places, in almost any soil or exposure.

Malus spp., flowering crab apple

Flowering crab apple grows in all regions, in almost any soil, including poor soil, but does need good drainage, and water during the dry periods. These trees, from 10–20 feet in height, are usually grown for their profuse handsome flowers, which appear before the leaves. The dark red fruits are attractive and useful in making preserves.

Morus rubra, red mulberry

This tree does well in all regions, but grows best in moist locations. However, the dropping fruits can be a nuisance on walks or lawns. The trees reach 25 to 30 feet in height and prefer moist soils.

Nyssa sylvatica, black tupelo, sourgum, black gum

This tree grows in the Appalachian mountains and the Piedmont to 60 feet in height, and prefers wet or swampy places, but it will grow even under poor conditions. Autumn coloration is vivid scarlet.

Oxydendrum arboreum, sourwood (Figure 22, 22a)

Sourwood grows in the Appalachian mountains and the Piedmont to an average of 35 feet, preferring full sun and sandy soils with organic matter. It is difficult to transplant.

Pinus palustris, white bark pine, longleaf pine

This pine grows in the Piedmont and the coastal plain and may reach 70 feet in height. The needles are extremely handsome, reaching a length of 12 inches or more. It does well in sun and well-drained soils.

Pinus pinaster, cluster pine

This pine tree, a native of the Mediterranean, usually reaches a height of 25 feet along the beaches. It does well on poor sand, but will do better if it is planted away from direct salt spray. An excellent evergreen tree, if planted in groups the trees should be spaced 10 feet apart.

22. *Oxydendrum arboreum,* sourwood (Photos courtesy U. S. Forest Service)

Pinus strobus, white pine

White pine grows in the lower elevations of the Appalachian mountains and the Piedmont from 50–75 feet in height. Easily transplanted, it is a commonly used landscape tree which can be pruned to keep it down to size for smaller properties. It will grow in rather poor conditions but thrives on rich organic soils. The younger trees are pyramidal and dense but with age they become flatter-topped.

Pinus taeda, loblolly pine

Found in the Piedmont and the coastal plain, this tree can grow to be over 70 feet in height. Suited for large properties. Prefers deep, moist soils, but will grow on dry soils.

Pinus thunbergii, Japanese black pine

This fast-growing pine usually only reaches 20 feet in height along the beaches. It is more resistant to salt spray than are our native pines. It is used in borders, for property lines, along driveways, and to form screens, when spaced about 6 feet apart. It may also be used as a specimen plant.

Pinus virginiana, scrub pine, Jersey pine, Virginia pine

Growing in all regions to 40 feet in height, this pine is grown where other pines would not survive, especially in very poor rocky soil.

Platanus occidentalis, sycamore, buttonwood

Growing in all regions to 75 feet in height, sycamore is a majestic tree that does best in rich organic soil. The peeling bark and the seed pods can clutter up a lawn.

Prunus caroliniana, Carolina cherry-laurel

The cherry-laurel grows in the coastal plain from 20 to 35 feet in height. It is grown for its evergreen leaves more than its flowers or fruits.

Prunus cerasifera, 'Pissardia,' Pissard plum

This tree grows in the Piedmont and the coastal plain to 25 feet in height. It is noted for its reddish-purple foliage, which requires good sunny exposure to develop. It withstands hot, dry weather.

Prunus serotina, wild black cherry, rum cherry

This widely distributed tree reaches 50 feet or more in height. It will grow on sandy as well as loam soils, and adjusts to sun and partial shade. It should be planted some distance from the ocean, as it is only partially resistant to salt spray. It is used as a specimen and for a shade tree, and the dark, gleaming black cherries attract birds. The leaves turn orange in the fall, and the midribs red.

Quercus alba, white oak

White oak grows in all regions to a height of 70 feet. It is a slow grower with widely spread branches. It needs up to 80 feet of space and is suited for large properties, as are many of the other oaks. It is not too selective about the soils it grows in but won't tolerate too much moisture. It can grow in sun and partial shade.

Quercus nigra, water oak

Water oak grows in the Piedmont and the coastal plain to 75 feet in height. It is easily transplanted and fast-growing, doing best on moist, well-drained soils in sun or partial shade.

Quercus palustris, pin oak, swamp oak, water oak

This oak grows in the Appalachian mountains and the Piedmont to 70 feet in height, and is considered the most beautiful of the oaks in shape. It will grow on moist, rich soil, but adapts to other soils as well.

Quercus phellos, willow oak

The willow oak grows in all regions to 60 feet in height, and is easily transplanted. The small willow-shaped leaves give it a very fine texture compared with other oaks. Early in its development it has a pyramidal shape which gradually becomes rounded. One of the most popular oaks, it tolerates wet soils better than other oaks, and grows in sandy as well as clay soils.

Quercus rubra, northern red oak

Northern red oak grows in the Piedmont and the Appalachian mountains to a height of 80 feet. Adapted to well-drained soils, it transplants easily, and is the most rapid-growing of the oaks, preferring rich, moist soils and partial shade. The tree's shape is handsome and the autumn coloration lovely.

Quercus virginiana, live oak
Live oak grows in the coastal plains to 50 feet in height, often very close to salt water. It transplants readily and grows fairly rapidly. The leaves are evergreen.

Robinia pseudoacacia, black locust, common locust
This tree grows in all regions to 30 feet in height. It will grow in poor, sterile, dry soils but does best on rich organic soils. It produces sprouts readily, and fragrant white flowers in clusters give rise to pods that remain on the tree over winter. It is subject to borer attacks.

Sassafras albidum, sassafras
Sassafras grows in the Appalachian mountains to 35 feet in height. Although it is difficult to transplant, it will grow in gravelly soils in partial shade or sun. It has brilliant red-orange colors in the fall.

Sorbus americana, mountain ash, rowan tree
American ash grows in the Appalachian mountains to a height of 20 feet, showing small white flowers in clusters, later producing orange to red fruits. This tree is short-lived, but will grow in rocky areas. It is subject to infestation by borers.

Taxodium distichum, bald cypress, common bald cypress
This tree grows in the coastal plain and Piedmont to 80 feet in height. It is adapted to dry areas as well as wet ones, and will even grow in standing water. It is noted for its knobby growths or knees near the base of the trunk. Though it is not recommended for small properties or urban properties, it is a fine specimen tree.

Taxus baccata, English yew, European yew
The yew tree grows in the Appalachian mountains to 40 or 50 feet in height and will grow in almost any soil. It is a slow grower and very long-lived. It will withstand constant pruning and can be used as a hedge. There are a large number of varieties available with a diversity of growth habits.

Tsuga canadensis, Canadian hemlock

This hemlock grows in the Appalachian mountains and the Piedmont to 90 feet in height or taller at higher altitudes. It is considered one of the best evergreen ornamentals because it is a slow grower and can be pruned regularly to any height or even as a hedge. It prefers moist, cool areas, adapts to shade, and to a wide range of soils.

Tsuga caroliniana, Carolina hemlock

Carolina hemlock grows best in the Appalachian mountains but is adapted to the Piedmont, and does well in urban areas. It can reach 75 feet in height but can be pruned to keep it lower.

Ulmus americana, American elm, white elm

This elm grows in all regions. It is a handsome, vase-shaped tree best liked for its shade. Although it will grow on wet soils, it does better on well-drained, rich soils. It will grow in partial shade.

RECOMMENDED REFERENCES

North Carolina Agricultural Extension Service, *Fruit Trees and Ornamental Budding and Grafting.* Extension Circular No. 326, North Carolina State University, Raleigh, N.C. 27607, April 1972.

————, *Trees for North Carolina.* Horticultural Information Leaflet No. 503, North Carolina State University, Raleigh, N.C. 27607.

U. S. Department of Agriculture, *Growing of Flowering Crabapples.* Home and Garden Bulletin No. 135, Washington, D.C. 20250, November 1967.

————, *Growing the Flowering Dogwood.* Home and Garden Bulletin No. 88, Washington, D.C. 20250, October 1971.

————, *Growing Hollies.* Home and Garden Bulletin No. 130, Washington, D.C. 20250, November 1967.

————, *Growing Magnolias.* Home and Garden Bulletin No. 132, Washington, D.C. 20250, July 1971.

————, *Trees for Shade and Beauty.* Home and Garden Bulletin No. 117, Washington, D.C. 20250, March 1972.

23. If planting is delayed shrubs and trees should be heeled
in as shown in the sketch. The trench is filled with soil
loosely packed. (Courtesy U. S. Department of Agriculture)

CHAPTER 6

Shrubs

The most practical description of a shrub is a woody plant with large numbers of lateral branches, lacking a central trunk, and reaching a height of 25 to 30 feet. However, the description is broad enough to make the distinction between a shrub and a tree in some cases rather difficult. Shrubs may be deciduous, shedding their leaves in the fall, or evergreen, keeping their foliage all year. Shrubs will occupy their part of the landscape scene for many years and it is advisable when planning for shrubs to have in mind their size five to ten years from planting, rather than their planting size.

Use

Shrubs can be used to define areas such as walkways, driveways, and areas in the landscape plan. They can be used to indicate property boundaries, provide privacy for barbecue and lounging areas, and to some degree, act as sound barriers. Some shrubs with spines such as pyracantha can be planted below ground level windows and kept pruned down to serve as an obstacle to intruders. We have used aucubas and camellias on a very steep hillside, with success.

The beauty of shrubs is shape and texture, flower and fruit, all of which add to the charm of a landscape plan. In addition, shrubs require modest care and are easy to maintain.

Buying Plants

Shrubs will be bought either bare-rooted, as are all roses, or with a ball of earth in a burlap wrapping. It is of the utmost importance that the roots do not dry out. If the plants have to be kept for a short time before planting, put them in a shaded area. The balled plants should be soaked; the bare-rooted plants can have their lower portions wrapped in wet burlap or newspapers, or can be "heeled" in a trench at an angle of 45 degrees (Figure 23).

Water is taken into a plant through the root hairs. Drying out can kill the root hairs, resulting in delayed growth or, in extreme cases, the death of the plant.

Planting Time

Shrubs bought with balls of earth can be planted from very early spring till late fall, but the earlier they go into the ground the better condition they will be in to take winter cold. However, they can be planted at other times as well, including the dormant season.

Bare-rooted plants do best planted from September to November, but can be planted on up to January or February. However, with good care and adequate watering they can be planted in other months as well.

Planting Methods

BARE ROOT

The hole for the bare-rooted plants should be at least a foot deeper than the roots and the width of the hole should be at least twice the diameter of the roots (Figure 24). Place the topsoil in one pile and the subsoil separately. When replacing the soil reverse order, so that the roots will be in contact with the richer topsoil. Add peat moss or decayed organic material, and one or two cups of superphosphate well mixed into the soil.

If the soil is not too wet, pack it around the roots of bare-rooted plants using your hands or a shovel handle, with caution.

A small earth dam can be mounded up about 2 feet from the stem to hold water near the plant to prevent drying out. A few handfuls of peat moss or organic matter in the dam will conserve moisture.

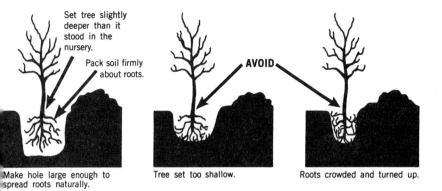

Set tree slightly deeper than it stood in the nursery.

Pack soil firmly about roots.

AVOID

Make hole large enough to spread roots naturally.

Tree set too shallow.

Roots crowded and turned up.

24. Planting procedure for a bare-rooted plant (Courtesy U. S. Department of Agriculture)

PRUNING

A general recommendation is to cut back the tops of newly planted bare-rooted plants to balance the usual damage done to roots in transplanting. The amount to prune will depend on the amount of root damage, but varies from one fourth to one third of the plant (Figure 25).

BALL AND CONTAINER

For balled plants dig a hole deep and wide enough to accept comfortably the ball of earth at the same level it was growing before lifting (Figure 26).

If the earth ball is in burlap make a few slits in the bag after it is in the planting hole. If any other container is used it must be removed very carefully at the edge of the hole, or in the hole in the case of clay pots, which can be broken in the hole. Tin cans are more trouble and should be removed by making vertical cuts or slits on both sides of the can and gently forcing the can open. Gloves are recommended.

Plant Site

The site for a particular shrub is a key to successful planting. Some plants thrive in direct sun, others do better in partial shade,

25. Pruning of bare-rooted plant after transplanting (Courtesy U. S. Department of Agriculture)

and some prefer deep shade. A plant in poor light conditions will fail to grow or will die.

Some of the traditional southern plants prefer high soil organic content, such as azaleas, camellias, and rhododendrons.

Abelia spp., abelia

Abelia grows in all regions, and does well in full sun or partial sun. If left unpruned, it will grow from 6 to 8 feet in height, but will withstand severe pruning and shaping and may be used as a hedge or border. Its pink-white flowers are borne on long stems. The leaves turn bronze in the autumn.

Arbutus unedo, strawberry tree

The strawberry tree grows in the Piedmont and the coastal plain in sun or partial shade and prefers a well-drained, loamy soil that is not neutral or slightly acid. This evergreen has white, showy, bell-like flowers.

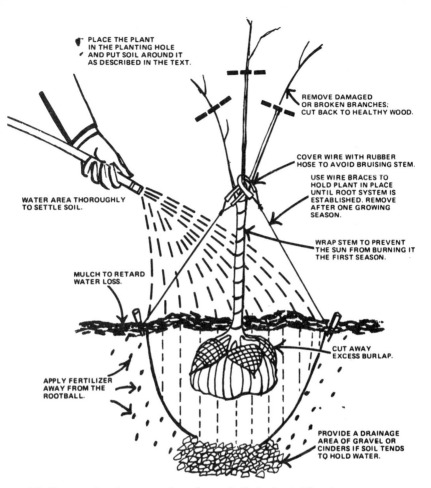

PLACE THE PLANT
IN THE PLANTING HOLE
AND PUT SOIL AROUND IT
AS DESCRIBED IN THE TEXT.

REMOVE DAMAGED
OR BROKEN BRANCHES;
CUT BACK TO HEALTHY WOOD.

COVER WIRE WITH RUBBER
HOSE TO AVOID BRUISING STEM.

USE WIRE BRACES TO
HOLD PLANT IN PLACE
UNTIL ROOT SYSTEM IS
ESTABLISHED. REMOVE
AFTER ONE GROWING
SEASON.

WATER AREA THOROUGHLY
TO SETTLE SOIL.

WRAP STEM TO PREVENT
THE SUN FROM BURNING IT
THE FIRST SEASON.

MULCH TO RETARD
WATER LOSS.

CUT AWAY
EXCESS BURLAP.

APPLY FERTILIZER
AWAY FROM THE
ROOTBALL.

PROVIDE A DRAINAGE
AREA OF GRAVEL OR
CINDERS IF SOIL TENDS
TO HOLD WATER.

26. Proper planting procedure for a balled plant (Courtesy
U. S. Department of Agriculture)

Aucuba japonica, aucuba, gold-dust

Aucuba grows in the Appalachian mountains and the Piedmont;
the coastal plain is too warm for it. It does best in a well-drained
but moist, rich soil preferably in partial or full shade. Some species
have white or yellow spots on the leaves. It produces a bright red
berry. It can grow to 6 feet or more in height.

Baccharis halimifolia, sea myrtle, salt bush, eastern baccharis

Growing to 10 feet in height in the Piedmont and the coastal plain,
this shrub can be used as a border, screen, or windbreak. The downy

thistle-shaped flowers appear in late fall or winter. It prefers a sunny location with adequate moisture and grows on beaches and sand dunes in moist areas. It is resistant to salt spray and even salt-water flooding, and is recommended in sand dunes as a barrier to protect less resistant plants. It can be grown from seed or cuttings under glass. Plants should be in double rows, 3 feet apart. It is not handsome, but utilitarian.

Berberis sargentiana, and others, barberry

One of the few barberry species adapted to the South, *Berberis sargentiana* grows in all regions to 6 feet in height in full sun or partial sun, and prefers a well-drained, fertile loam. It is noted for its shiny, bright green leaves and its bright yellow flowers, and is used for hedges or borders.

Buxus sempervirens, and *B. microphylla,* boxwood

Boxwood grows in all regions in a range of soils, and requires cool, moist conditions. It is used for foundations, hedges, and borders, and to mark off areas. It responds well to pruning.

Callistemon spp., bottle brush

Bottle brush grows in the coastal plain on dry soil and is noted for its red spikes of flowers resembling laboratory bottle brushes. There are many species, all resembling each other, all imported from Australia.

Camellia japonica, camellia

Camellia grows in the Piedmont and the coastal plain, in partial or full sun, in a well-drained, acid soil. Plants must be protected from alternate freezing and thawing in order to bloom properly; a mulch and in extreme cases wrapping of the plants may be needed.

Cleyera japonica, cleyera, sakaki

Sakaki grows in the Piedmont and the coastal plain in partial shade or full sun and requires a well-drained, loamy, rich soil. It is noted for its fragrant, small white flowers, and its bright red berries during winter. There is a variegated variety with yellow and red leaves.

Cotoneaster spp., cotoneaster

Many species of cotoneaster are available, some evergreen, some deciduous, some dwarf, others shrubs.

Cotoneaster grows in all regions in partial or full sun, in a well-drained, loamy soil. Some species spread almost prostrate while others grow to about 10 feet in height. It is noted for its small pink flowers in early summer and its dark red berries in winter. (For use of the dwarf types as ground covers see Chapter 13.)

Elaeagnus pungens, thorny elaeagnus

This evergreen shrub grows in all regions and reaches 15 feet in height. It is distinguished by its wide shape resulting from the drooping of branches in a broad radius. Its gray and silver foliage, small fragrant flowers, and red berries add to its appeal. It will grow in full sun to partial shade in any well-drained soil, is highly resistant to salt spray, and can be used directly along the ocean front, planted 2 feet apart as a hedge, or 3–4 feet apart as a screen or barrier along the ocean for other plants.

Eriobotrya japonica, loquat (Figure 27)

An evergreen which grows in the Piedmont and the coastal plain, in well-drained, moist loam, in the sun, to 20 feet in height. The small white flowers appear from late summer to early winter, with the yellow fruits ripening in winter or early spring.

Euonymus spp., euonymus

Euonymus grows in all regions to 10 feet in height. *E. patens,* spreading euonymus, is generally preferred because *E. japonicus,* evergreen euonymus, is more susceptible to the euonymus scale. It is noted for its heavy flower clusters and red fall berries. It likes well-drained, rich, loamy soil in full sun, and requires regular spraying to protect against scale infestation.

The evergreen euonymus is preferred along the coast because it is very resistant to salt spray. As a barrier for other plants it is spaced 3–4 feet apart, as a shrub border 4 feet apart, or as a trimmed hedge 2 feet apart.

Fatsia japonica, Japanese fatsia (Figure 28)

A shrub used along the coastal plains, usually growing 3 to 6 feet

27. *Eriobotrya japonica,* loquat (Photo courtesy U. S. Forest Service)

in height on the ocean. This shrub, whose leaves have 7–9 lobes, will grow in poor soils in almost full shade. Since it is only partially resistant to salt spray it should have some protection. It is usually planted as specimens, small groups, or borders.

Gardenia jasminoides, and *G. thunbergia,* Cape jasmine
Cape jasmine grows in all regions to 6 feet in height, and requires a mildly acid, moist soil with partial shade. It is distinguished by shiny evergreen leaves and the heavily fragrant flowers appearing May to June.

Gordonia lasianthus, loblolly bay
An evergreen adapted to the coastal plain, loblolly bay requires a

moist soil and can grow to 30 or 60 feet in height. The leaves are bright green˙above and silver underneath, flowers fragrant, white, and 2 inches across.

Hesperaloe parviflora, red yucca

A native of the Southwest, red yucca grows in the coastal plain and preferably on a light loam with full sun or partial shade. The rose-red flowers are borne on 2½ to 4-foot-long flower stalks.

Ilex spp., hollies

Hollies prefer a well-drained, neutral to slightly acid loam, fairly light and sandy. Only the female trees bear berries. They are usually propagated from cuttings taken from the female trees to ensure bearing trees. There is no way to distinguish between the male and female trees until flowering occurs. These are all evergreens varying in size.

28. *Fatsia japonica,* Japanese fatsia (Photo courtesy Soil Conservation Service)

Ilex cornuta, Chinese holly

Chinese holly grows in the Piedmont and the coastal plain to 35 feet in height. If the soil is too dry and sandy, a mulch should be added. It is relatively insect- and disease-free. Because of its dense growth it is often used as a hedge.

Ilex crenata, Japanese holly

Japanese holly grows in all regions to 20 feet in height, and is used for hedges and screens.

Ilex glabra, inkberry, winterberry

This black-fruited holly does well in the coastal plain, in swampy areas, and in pine barrens, as well as in the lowlands, growing to 8 feet in height. It does well in sun and partial shade.

Illicium anisatum, anise tree

This shrub, growing to 9 feet in height or more, is best used in large borders. It grows in all regions on slightly acid, well-drained, rich soil, in partial shade. It is noted for its light green evergreen leaves that smell like anise, and has yellow-green flowers that lack fragrance.

Juniperus chinensis, 'Pfitzeriana,' Pfitzer juniper

This broad, flat-topped, pyramidal bluish evergreen grows to 5 feet in height. Only the female plants fruit. It will grow in rather poor soils and requires pruning once a year since it tends to become straggly. It is used in groups, borders, foundation plantings, and for mass plantings. It may be propagated from hardwood cuttings taken from September to December, which should be planted in a mixture of sand and peat moss.

Kalmia latifolia, mountain laurel, calico bush (Figure 29)

Mountain laurel grows in the Appalachian mountains and the Piedmont. It prefers a rich, moist, acid soil with partial shade, and with pruning is suitable for containers on a patio. This evergreen is noted for its white or pink spring flowers. The seed may be planted in February in peat moss in a warm place.

Leiophyllum buxifolium and *L. lyonii,* sand myrtle

These are low-growing evergreen shrubs. *L. buxifolium,* used as a hedge and specimen, is adapted to the Appalachian mountains,

29. *Kalmia latifolia,* mountain laurel (Photo courtesy U. S. Forest Service)

Piedmont, and somewhat less to the coast. *L. lyonii* is a prostrate form often planted in beach areas on dunes. It is salt-spray-resistant.

Leucothoe catesbaei, leucothoe

Leucothoe grows in the Appalachian mountains and the Piedmont, preferably in rich, moist, acid soil in a shady location, to 6 feet in height. The long dark green leaves turn red during winter. The white bell-shaped flowers are most attractive. It is a nice specimen plant.

Ligustrum japonicum, Japanese privet

This evergreen shrub grows in all regions to a height of 10 feet. It will tolerate shade and is drought-resistant. It can be grown from seed planted in the fall, or from cuttings taken from the growth tips in the summer, or from hardwood cuttings taken in winter or early spring. If used as a hedge it is usually spaced 2 feet apart; as a screen border, 3–4 feet apart. It is somewhat salt-spray-resistant, although it does better if it is protected from direct winds.

Ligustrum lucidum, glossy privet

Glossy privet grows in the Piedmont and the coastal plains to a height of 15 feet. The leaves are larger and more pointed than in *L. japonicum,* and the two may often be confused. Relatively free from insects and disease, it is the tallest-growing of the privets.

Ligustrum ovalifolium, California privet

This privet is used most often along the coast, for it is somewhat resistant to salt spray. Used as a hedge it is spaced 1½ feet apart.

Ligustrum vulgare, European privet

This semi-evergreen grows to 15 feet in height and is the most resistant of all privets to salt spray. It is used as a barrier to protect other plants from salt spray. As a border or screen it is planted 3 to 5 feet apart, as a clipped hedge it is usually spaced 2 feet between plants.

Mahonia bealei, leatherleaf, holly-grape

Leatherleaf grows in all regions in rich, moist, well-drained soil in partial to dense shade. It is noted for its small yellow flowers and its blue berries.

Michelia fuscata, banana shrub

The banana shrub grows to 15 feet in height in the coastal plain in rich, well-drained loam in full sun to partial shade. It can be pruned to remain smaller. The yellow, tulip-shaped flowers smell like bananas. The plant is an evergreen, and is used as a specimen.

Myrica cerifera, wax myrtle

Wax myrtle grows in the Piedmont and the coastal plains to 10 feet in height, in partial shade or sun in a wide variety of soils. It has dark green foliage and gray waxy berries. The male and female plants are separate. Cuttings may be taken in the spring and summer. The suckers may also be dug and transplanted. Seeds with the wax removed are planted in the fall. A spacing of 5 to 6 feet between plants is recommended.

Myrica pensylvanica, northern bayberry

This semi-evergreen shrub grows from 3 to 8 feet in height, is very resistant to salt spray, and will grow in poor sandy soils from dunes to marshes. It is recommended for use as a salt-spray barrier or screen; as a border plants are spaced 2 to 3 feet apart. It is recommended as a conservation plant more than a landscape plant.

Nandina domestica, heavenly bamboo

This shrub will grow in all regions to a height of 8 feet. Its leaves are vivid red in winter, and bright green in summer. White flowers produce large clusters of bright red berries which remain hanging all winter. This evergreen is non-branching and the new shoots grow from the roots; new growth is encouraged by cutting older stems back to ground level.

Nerium oleander, oleander

Oleander grows in the coastal plains to 20 feet in height, in almost any soil, and withstands hot, dry locations. It is used for borders, windbreaks, and screens. It is resistant to salt spray and is recommended as a salt-spray barrier, planted 4 feet apart. It is evergreen.

Osmanthus americanus, tea olive, wild olive, devilwood osmanthus, devilwood, devilwood olive

An evergreen growing in all regions to 20 feet in height. It prefers a well-drained, neutral to slightly acid, sandy loam, either in full sun or partial shade. It can be planted and pruned as a hedge. It is partially resistant to salt spray and grows well in poor sands but its main use is for foundation or specimen planting.

Photinia serrulata, Chinese photinia

Chinese photinia grows in all regions to a height of 30 feet and prefers a well-drained soil with plenty of moisture, in full sun to partial shade. It is used for mass plantings and large screens. It looks best with heavy pruning, as it tends to produce long shoots. *P. glabra* is adapted to sunny locations in the Piedmont and may grow to 10 feet in height.

Pieris floribunda, pieris

This evergreen grows in the Appalachian mountains in partial shade but will flower better in a sunny location. It does best in a moderately rich soil. This evergreen grows to 4 feet in height and 9 feet broad. The small white flowers grow in hanging clusters. Another species, *P. japonica,* will grow much taller.

Pittosporum tobira, tobira, pittosporum

This evergreen grows in the coastal plains to 10 feet in height and prefers rich, well-drained, loose soil in full sun, although it will grow in complete shade. It is suitable for formal gardens, hedges, and foundation plantings. The thick dark green leaves grow in whorls on the tips of the branches. It is very resistant to salt spray, and is spaced 3 feet apart for barriers and 4 feet for borders and screens.

Pyracantha angustifolia, firethorn, pyracantha

Firethorn grows in the Appalachian mountains and the Piedmont. It is used for specimens, for foundations and for walls and fences, for mass plantings, and under windows as burglar protection. It is liked because of its vigorous growth. Heavy pruning is not recommended since this limits the fruiting. However, frost-killed parts should be pruned in the spring. The flowers have a slightly unpleasant odor in the spring.

Raphiolepis indica, Japanese hawthorn, India hawthorn

R. indica grows in the Appalachian mountains and the Piedmont in well-drained soil, either in full sun or partial shade, and is somewhat drought-resistant. It grows to 4 feet in height and produces pinkish-white flowers that give rise to black cherries later in the season.

Raphiolepis umbellata, Yeddo raphiolepis

This evergreen shrub grows to 8 feet in height and is very resistant to salt spray. It is used for borders and foundation plantings and as a spray barrier on beaches. It requires a well-drained soil. A dwarf variety about 1 foot tall is available. It can be layered, and propagated by cuttings and seeds.

Rhododendron calendulaceum, flame azalea

This favorite grows in all regions to a height of 10 feet or more. The flowers range from yellow to orange or red, and are about 2

30. *Rhododendron catawbiense,* purple rhododendron (Photo courtesy U. S. Forest Service)

inches across. It prefers shade, but will do fairly well in the sun. Rich, acid loams are preferred.

Rhododendron carolinianum (Carolina rhododendron) and *R. catawbiense* (purple rhododendron) (Figure 30)

These grow in the Appalachian mountains in partial shade in well-drained, organic, acid soil. These are noted for large leathery leaves and giant clusters of vivid flowers. We refer to the mostly evergreen species here, and we use azalea for the mostly deciduous related plants.

Rhododendron maximum, great laurel

The great laurel is a shrub or small tree of the Appalachian mountains, the hardiest of the evergreen rhododendrons, and prefers shade to semi-shade. It requires moist growing conditions. The flowers are light pink.

ROSES

Because roses are probably the most popular garden flowers, we are including a special section (Figure 31). Each year new varieties appear to tempt the homeowner. The uses to which roses can be put are limited only by the amount of space available. Symbol of love as well as sympathy, the rose has been involved in man's affairs for a long, long time.

Kinds of Roses

BUSH

Hybrid tea. These are the most popular of roses, everblooming, growing as tall as 5 or 6 feet. The flowers vary from a single one to a stem to clusters of five, and come in a range of colors and varying stem length. Most are fragrant.

Floribundas produce flower clusters in great numbers.

Grandifloras bear single blooms on long stems and are strong bloomers.

Polyanthas bear small flowers in large clusters on small, compact plants. They are well suited for beds and borders.

Hybrid perpetuals have large flowers, often doubles, and are vigorous, upright growers. They bear over a long period but not as long as do the hybrid tea roses.

Miniature roses. These have tiny flowers on tiny plants, some growing to 6 inches at maturity. They are suited for use in rock gardens, borders, and potted specimens.

Tree roses are usually found in formal gardens or large properties. Bush-type roses are grafted onto upright trunks.

Old-fashioned roses are descendants of the roses of colonial times. In this group are the white York and pink Lancaster roses, made famous in the Wars of the Roses. These are usually strongly fragrant.

CLIMBING ROSES

Ramblers are rapid-growing, bearing small flowers in large clusters. Flowering is limited to one-year-old canes, which may reach 20 feet in one growing season.

Climbing roses produce long canes and require a trellis or other

31. A good many roses for garden centers are being grown in the United States. Here in Salt River Valley near Phoenix is Arnold Krochmal at a Jackson-Perkins rose farm.

support. They are useful to hide fences and on slopes to reduce erosion. There are a number of varieties.

Culture

Roses require at least six hours of full sunlight a day and will adapt to a wide range of soils. Good drainage is essential, and if a site does not meet this requirement it should be dug out and the soil replaced.

Annual pruning is a necessity to ensure good blooming. Weak varieties are pruned less than strong-growing varieties. The length and number of shoots are reduced.

Principal disease problems are fungal in origin, including mildew, black spot canker, plus bacterial crown gall. These are discussed in the chapter on diseases.

Insect pests include aphids, thrips, leaf hoppers, rose chafers, rose scales, Japanese beetles, leaf beetles, and spider mites.

For both insects and disease pre-mixed rose dusts and sprays are available in garden shops.

We mulch our roses heavily with pine bark, and sometimes use peat moss as well. Dried cow manure worked into the soil in the spring, plus 2 pounds of an 8–8–8 fertilizer per 100 square feet is an excellent fertilizer program for roses. Fall or spring planting is satisfactory.

Tamarix gallica, French tamarisk, salt cedar

This graceful shrub grows to 10 feet in height and is resistant to salt spray and winds. It can be used as a salt-spray barrier with plants spaced 3 feet apart. It should not be planted near other plants or near a house because the branches whipping in the wind can be damaging.

Thea sinensis, tea

Tea grows in the coastal plain in light shade in a slightly acid, well-drained, rich, loose soil. This evergreen is noted for its white fragrant flowers, which bloom in late fall. It is to be seen at Charles Towne Landing and is the source of the beverage tea.

Umbellularia californica, California laurel, California bay

An evergreen with fragrant leaves, California laurel grows in the coastal plain in sunny locations in well-drained loam. It may grow to 30 or 50 feet in height.

Viburnum spp., viburnum

Species grow in the Piedmont and the Appalachian mountains in well-drained, rich loam. There are evergreen and deciduous species. They have white-pinkish flowers that bloom in late winter or very early spring. There are over one hundred species. A species can be found for almost any soil type and light condition.

Yucca spp., yucca

Yuccas are very resistant to salt spray, and some species will grow in dry sandy soils. They usually are used as borders.

Yucca aloifolia, Spanish dagger

The trunk can grow to 10 feet in height.

Yucca filamentosa, Adam's-needle, beargrass

This yucca grows in the coastal plain with leaves 1 to 2 feet in height and no trunk. Its white bell-like flowers appear from May to June. It spreads by tubers.

Yucca gloriosa, mound-lily yucca

This yucca's trunk can grow to 15 feet in height.

Zanthoxylum clava-herculis, Hercules' club, prickly ash

This shrub grows to 12 feet in height, along beach areas. It is very resistant to salt spray and will grow in the sand. It is used as salt-spray barriers, untrimmed hedges, or as background borders, spaced 5 to 7 feet apart.

RECOMMENDED REFERENCES

Clemson University Extension Service, *Azaleas in South Carolina.* Circular 508, Clemson, S.C., May 1972.

North Carolina Agricultural Extension Service, *Boxwood Troubles.* Horticultural Information Leaflet No. 422, North Carolina State University, Raleigh, N.C. 27607, March 1970.

————, *Poinsettias—Care and Handling.* Horticultural Information Leaflet No. 525, North Carolina State University, Raleigh, N.C. 27607, January 1967.

————, *Roses.* Folder 104, North Carolina State University, Raleigh, N.C. 27607, May 1971.

————, *Successful Rose Culture.* Circular 200, North Carolina State University, Raleigh, N.C. 27607, June 1969.

U. S. Department of Agriculture, *Growing Azaleas and Rhododendrons.* Home and Garden Bulletin No. 71, Washington, D.C. 20250, 1972.

————, *Growing Boxwood.* Home and Garden Bulletin No. 120, Washington, D.C. 20250, July 1971.

————, *Growing Gardenias.* Home and Garden Bulletin No. 152, Washington, D.C. 20250, January 1971.

————, *Roses for the Home.* Home and Garden Bulletin No. 25, Washington, D.C. 20250, January 1972.

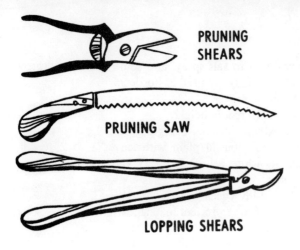

PRUNING SHEARS

PRUNING SAW

LOPPING SHEARS

32. Pruning tools (Courtesy U. S. Department of Agriculture)

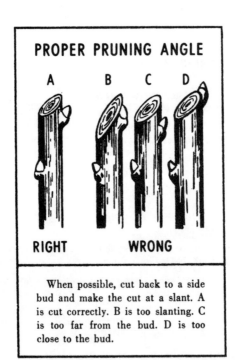

PROPER PRUNING ANGLE

A   B   C   D

RIGHT   **WRONG**

When possible, cut back to a side bud and make the cut at a slant. A is cut correctly. B is too slanting. C is too far from the bud. D is too close to the bud.

33. Proper pruning angle to aim growth in the direction wanted (Courtesy U. S. Department of Agriculture)

CHAPTER 7

Pruning Shrubs and Trees

SHRUBS

Purposes

Pruning is used to shape plants, control their size, remove crowded, rubbing, and diseased branches, encourage flowering, strengthen the structure, and protect plant health. We can divide shrubs into two major classes: evergreens which hold their leaves all year, and deciduous shrubs which drop their leaves in the fall.

Tools

There are three basic tools the home gardener needs to prune (Figure 32). These are pruning shears, a pruning saw, and lopping shears.

Lopping shears are best for thick branches and can be used for reaching into a tree or shrub. Hand shears are fine for small branches, twigs, and vines. Both tools should be kept sharp and oiled; and when used the cut should be hard and straight without twisting.

The pruning saw is used for larger branches than the lopping shears can handle.

In using these tools, the method of cutting (Figure 33) is of major importance. The best cut is at an angle to a side bud, not too close to the bud, and not too far, and not at too sharp a slant.

Cuts made in limbs over 1 inch in diameter should be covered with an asphalt wound dressing available at garden stores and nurseries.

Additional tools may be useful. We like a pole pruner to get to the top of taller shrubs we want to head back. When a larger shrub dies or must be removed a small power saw can be rented, *but use with care!* To cut down a shrub start with limbs and work your way down the trunk.

EVERGREEN SHRUBS

Evergreens can be separated into two types: the broad-leaved, which include azalea, box, holly, and mountain laurel, and the cone-bearing, needle-leaved types such as pine, fir, juniper, and arborvitae.

Broad-leaved Evergreens

Old inflorescence of broad-leaved evergreens which go into dormancy with flower buds formed and plump should be pruned right after flowering in the spring. Azalea and rhododendron are examples of broad-leaved evergreens.

Those shrubs that produce flowers on the current year's growth may be pruned during the dormant season. If they bear fruits they can be pruned after the fruit ripens. Spiraea, althaea, crape myrtle, and everblooming roses are included here.

Broad-leaved evergreens can be kept a desired size by annual pruning of new growth and some thinning of new or old growth, as well as by cutting excess shoots out entirely (Figure 34).

Plants used as hedges should be trimmed as frequently as good shaping requires.

When pruning always cut back to a bud or green shoot growing in the direction you select for development.

Conifers

Cone-bearing evergreens are pruned from March to May when shoots and buds are newly formed. If annual pruning is practiced, cutting should be confined to pruning back enough new growth to produce the desired shape and size. If branches require major pruning cut them back to a shoot just after spring growth begins. A number of methods to aid in shaping conifers are used (Figure 35).

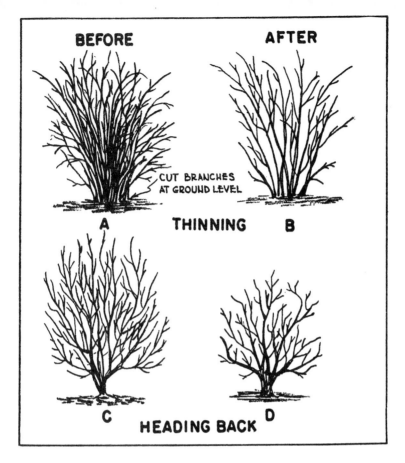

34. Pruning and thinning (Courtesy U. S. Department of Agriculture)

Hedges should be trimmed as needed to maintain their vigor and desired shape.

Cone-bearing evergreens may be kept to a suitable size by two methods. One requires pruning of the roots by digging around the trunk under the outer tips or drip, of the trees, with a spade. Plants that are adapted to such treatment include firs, pines, junipers, and cedar. Another method used to keep evergreens short and compact requires the pruning back of the leader, or main shoot. If two leaders are present remove the weaker and prune back the other.

Prune pines in late spring by removing one-half of the candle, or new shoot. Do not damage needle tips because the tips of cut needles tend to turn brown.

You can reduce open spaces on spruces by cutting off one-half of the leader, or terminal shoot, in the spring when the new needles are about half developed.

Keep side branches from growing out of bounds by removing the terminal bud. This not only slows outward growth but also helps to make the plants more bushy.

You can replace a lost leader by tying one of the branches in the top whorl to a vertical brace.

Trees that have already grown too wide can be narrowed by cutting the branches back to an inner bud.

If the tree develops two leaders, remove the less desirable one in early spring. Trees with more than one leader are weaker and less attractive than trees that have a single, strong, central leader.

35. Pruning of conifers (Courtesy U. S. Department of Agriculture)

DECIDUOUS SHRUBS

Deciduous shrubs can be pruned at any time of the year. Quite often if we find a shrub growing more than we want it to grow, or in a direction we hadn't planned for it, we prune it right then and there. As we write this chapter, in late August, we have just removed a number of large, drooping shoots from several forsythias growing much longer than we had planned.

If pruning for a particular shape or direction of growth is desired be sure to prune back to a bud or shoot "aimed" in the direction you are encouraging growth.

When cutting back to a bud, the cut should be made even with the top of the bud. When cutting a branch make the cut against the trunk without a stub (Figure 36). If you prune out dead branches cut an inch or two into live wood.

Size can be controlled by pruning straggly branches, which are cut back to larger, more attractive branches, or back to the stem on young shrubs.

Spring-flowering Shrubs

The flowers of many shrubs that bloom in the spring are borne on the previous year's growth. The best time to prune spring bloomers is right after full bloom in the spring. If winter pruning is used many flower buds will be removed and the bloom reduced the next spring.

Some of the spring bloomers are azalea, dogwood, elder, pyracantha, forsythia, honeysuckle, mock orange, and viburnum.

Summer-flowering Shrubs

Summer-blooming shrubs bear their flowers on the current year's growth and should be pruned during the dormant season before growth begins in the spring. Included in this category are abelia, crape myrtle, hydrangea, magnolia, mint shrub, rose, spiraea, and hibiscus.

VINES

Without pruning vines could overrun a garden and wreak havoc with other plantings. The amount of pruning will depend on the growth rate of the vine.

36. A—branch to be pruned
    B—stub left too long
    C—maximum stub length that is considered satisfactory
    D—maximum cut that is considered satisfactory
(Photo courtesy U. S. Department of Agriculture)

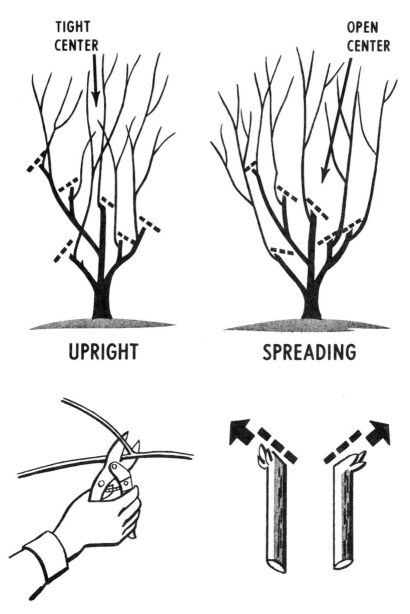

TIGHT CENTER

OPEN CENTER

UPRIGHT

SPREADING

To change the shape of a plant, cut it back to where a branch or twig grows in the direction you want the plant to grow.

You can control the direction of the new growth by cutting back to a side bud that points in the direction you want the branch to grow. New growth will follow the dotted line.

37. Pruning of an open-center and a tight-center shrub (Courtesy U. S. Department of Agriculture)

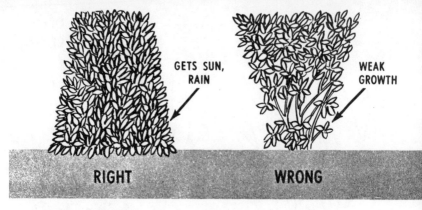

RIGHT — GETS SUN, RAIN

WRONG — WEAK GROWTH

38. Hedge pruning (Courtesy U. S. Department of Agriculture)

All vines except flowering clematis are pruned in the dormant season or as needed. Clematis is pruned in the spring after flowering.

SPECIAL PRUNING METHODS

To make a shrub shorter and more compact excess branches should be pruned out at ground level. If you are trying to prune back a shoot to direct growth in a particular direction cut back to a bud or a shoot growing in the direction you have in mind. An open-center shrub can be produced by pruning a number of branches growing inward. A shrub with a tight, compact center can be produced by pruning some of the shoots growing away from the center (Figure 37).

To prune hedges, a flat top flaring outward gradually to the bottom serves best by exposing more of the plant to sunlight. To produce a formal shrub as part of a hedge, or as a specimen, pruning twigs close is recommended. An informal effect can be created by keeping pruning to a minimum (Figure 38).

Sometimes a shrub will present a straggly, overgrown appearance. To shape such a shrub to appear more attractive prune up to one half of the shoots at ground level. A shrub that has become too tall can be headed back by cutting the taller shoots back, as well as by removing some of the shoots (Figure 39).

Flower set as well as size of flowers can be increased the following year by removing flowers after full bloom, the tips of shoots that have failed to flower, and the seed pods (Figure 40). Both seeds and flowers absorb large amounts of plant foods. Their removal allows

RIGHT

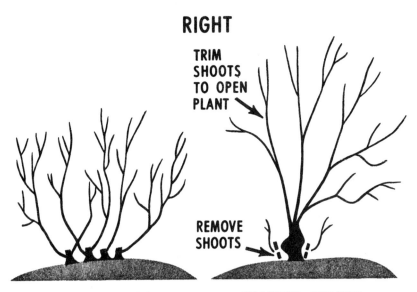

TRIM SHOOTS TO OPEN PLANT

REMOVE SHOOTS

OLD SHRUBS

To prune old shrubs, cut the old stems back to the point where the branches originate, near the ground.

GRAFTED SHRUBS

When pruning shrubs that have been grafted, always remove new twigs that start below the graft knuckle.

WRONG

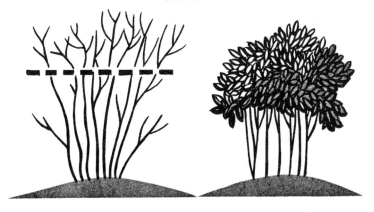

When shrubs are beheaded, as at left, new growth comes only from the top of the plant, resulting in the leggy, bushy-topped shrub shown at the right.

39. Proper pruning of overgrown shrub (Courtesy U. S. Department of Agriculture)

SHAPING PLANTS

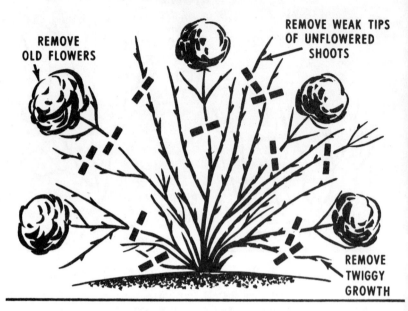

REMOVE
OLD FLOWERS

REMOVE WEAK TIPS
OF UNFLOWERED
SHOOTS

REMOVE
TWIGGY
GROWTH

REMOVING SEED PODS

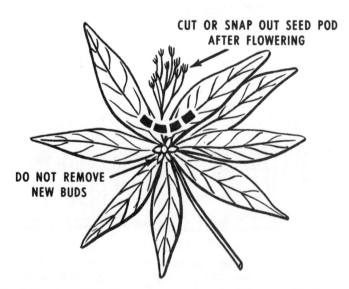

CUT OR SNAP OUT SEED POD
AFTER FLOWERING

DO NOT REMOVE
NEW BUDS

40. Removing dead flowers and seed pods (Courtesy U. S.
Department of Agriculture)

the plant foods to be stored in the plant and used for increased flowering next season.

TREES

Purposes

The principles used in the pruning of trees are essentially the same as for shrubs. Early pruning of damaged and diseased branches can save work later on.

In pruning trees remove shoots growing at the base of the tree, branches growing in toward the center of the tree, V crotches, crossed and rubbing branches, and branches that rub against the roof or other parts of the house and against power and phone lines, and limbs blocking your view.

Needle-leaf Evergreens

Arborvitae and similar evergreens are sheared overall to give them a desired shape. Pines and similar plants are best shaped by pruning limbs and those parts that have objectionable growth features.

If dense growth is desired in a pine or a pine-like evergreen prune back the young, immature "candle growth," which will encourage small-branch development. For the same dense effect, cut branches back to a smaller fork in the spring, removing the growth of the previous year. New branches will begin to develop.

Broad-leaf Trees

The first cut in stub-cutting is made about 1 foot out on the limb by sawing upward halfway through the limb. This will prevent the bark from tearing down the trunk when the final cut is made.

Next make a cut a few inches out from the first cut and cut through the limb.

In general, when pruning a limb, prune back to the trunk (Figure 41) because a stub is both unattractive and can serve as an entrance for diseases.

A V crotch is a source of great structural weakness and must be eliminated by pruning out one branch. This should be done in a way that leaves the stub at an angle of 30 to 45 degrees to present the smallest possible area to disease invasion and a minimum area for water to soak in.

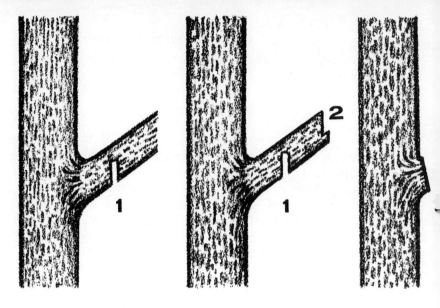

41. In cutting a large branch care should be used to avoid splitting the wood and peeling the bark. First make a cut from below (1), then cut the limb from above (2), and finally remove the stub with a clean cut (3). (Courtesy U. S. Department of Agriculture)

Treating Wounds

Cuts over 1 inch in diameter should be covered with a wound preparation available at a nursery or garden store. The dressing should remain covered, and replaced if the coating cracks or pulls.

Needle-leaf evergreens secrete resins and gums which often cover a wound and protect it as well as a commercial preparation. If these natural materials are sparse or not present, then a commercial coating should be used.

Flowering and Fruiting Trees

Some trees are grown for the ornamental value of their fruits and flowers. Among these are one group which requires spring pruning after flowering is complete. These trees produce flower buds one summer for the *following* year's flowers. Pruning these in the fall reduces the following flower crop. In this class are dogwood, flowering crab apple, and spring-blooming magnolia.

Holly is best pruned in the early spring or early winter in December. Pruning too many ripe fruits can reduce the following year's crop.

To increase rhododendron blooms pinch off dying flowers and the entire spur on which the flowers grow. This will increase bud formation. Flower formation in the magnolia can be encouraged by removing dying flowers.

RECOMMENDED REFERENCES

North Carolina Agricultural Extension Service, *Pruning Shrubs.* Extension Folder 215, North Carolina State University, Raleigh, N.C. 27607, March 1970.

————, *Pruning Trees and Shrubs.* Horticultural Information Leaflet No. 427, North Carolina State University, Raleigh, N.C. 27607, October 1970.

U. S. Department of Agriculture, *Pruning Ornamental Shrubs and Vines.* Home and Garden Bulletin No. 165, Washington, D.C. 20250, March 1969.

————, *Pruning Shade Trees and Repairing Their Injuries.* Home and Garden Bulletin No. 83, Washington, D.C. 20250, October 1970.

CHAPTER 8

Propagation

There are two practical means of producing new plants. One is by sexual methods, using seeds, and the other by vegetative or asexual methods, using parts of an older plant. Each method has advantages and disadvantages.

Using home-produced seeds for annuals will be a chancy practice. The problem is less serious for trees, shrubs, and perennials. If a plant is *self-pollinated,* the seeds will give rise to plants resembling the parent plant. However, if the plant is *cross-pollinated,* as many plants are, there is a possibility of crossing with other varieties of the species, and in such a case the seeds would produce plants different than the parent plant. Because of the large variety of annuals, accidental hybrids might be very undesirable. Although some gardening enthusiasts deliberately make crosses to create new varieties, as a hobby, the average gardener will not become involved in this activity and should buy seeds from a reputable source to avoid accidental hybrids.

PLANTS FROM SEED

Protected Sites

Gardeners can start seeds several weeks before they will need plants for setting out of doors by using a suitable area of the home such as a bright, warm room; also, an electric gardening setup, hot-beds, or cold frames. Sketches for hotbeds and cold frames are available from the Extension Horticulturist at Clemson University and North Carolina State University.

Outdoors

For direct seeding outdoors, which usually means later flowering, a suitable area should be prepared the previous fall. The soil must be worked up well, organic material and fertilizer added if needed. At planting time rows can be marked with string, and shallow furrows made.

We usually cover seeds with vermiculite a thickness two times their own diameter, and water carefully to keep from washing the vermiculite and the seeds away.

Collecting Seeds

Seeds should be harvested when the flowers, capsules, or fruits are ripe. The drying of flowers is one sign of maturity. In other cases, such as the persimmon, the fruit drops to the ground and can be harvested then. The dogwood fruits turn a bright red.

When dried flowers are harvested for seed they can be gently rubbed between the palms and the seeds screened or picked out by hand.

Pulpy fruits can be put into a bucket of water and the fruits macerated in the water by hand to loosen the seed. Pouring off the water, separating and drying the seeds in a shady spot with ventilation will complete the procedure. Seeds in small fruits, such as poke-berry, can be separated easily by using a colander to crush the fruit. The seeds are then dried as described above. Seeds in capsules, and nuts, require opening the hulls or pods and extraction of seeds from the chaff.

Buying seeds will eliminate all of this effort, if seeds are available, but for many wild plants, extraction is usually the only method to obtain the seed.

Containers

Seeds can be planted in pots, plant bands, and seed flats. Those which transplant readily can be sown in seed flats or pots; those which do not transplant well should be planted in plant bands, as they can be placed directly in the garden, bands and all, with no disturbance to the roots.

Pots can be of clay or plastic, with a few rocks or broken crockery placed in the bottom to keep the soil from running out; plastic or wooden seed flats are used with a few sheets of newspaper in the bottom of the seed flats to keep the soil in place.

Plant bands come in a range of materials, square or round, and in different sizes. They are made of materials which disintegrate in the soil.

Soil Mixture

River sand, peat moss, vermiculite, and soil are used in varying proportions to make a potting mixture. Each plant grower has some particular formula his own experience suggests is the best for his needs. A basic formula might include equal amounts of each ingredient.

If the gardener should want to sterilize small amounts of soil, a practice that helps control soil-borne organisms and weed seeds, soil can be placed in an oven in a metal container and baked at 180° F. for thirty minutes with occasional stirring of the soil. When it has cooled the other ingredients can be added. Be cautious, as the hot soil can cause burns.

Planting Seeds

The soil mixture should be dampened, and the containers filled, firming the soil down well, particularly around the edges, using the thumbs.

In seed flats, mark rows with the edge of a planting stake, piece of wood, or some convenient item. If seeds from a package are being used, tap the open bag with the forefinger into the marked rows. For pots and bands use the same method.

The seeds should then be covered lightly with vermiculite. Very small seeds can be left uncovered. Very carefully sprinkle or bottom-irrigate by setting the planted container into another container with 1 or 2 inches of water, until the surface of the planted container is damp. Then cover with polyethylene sheets (Figure 42), or if small enough place in a polyethylene bag and store in a warm place until the seeds germinate.

When germination takes place, remove the plastic covering and

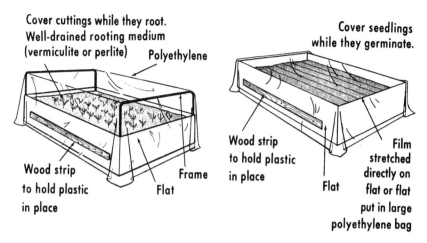

Cover cuttings while they root.
Well-drained rooting medium
(vermiculite or perlite)   Polyethylene

Cover seedlings
while they germinate.

Wood strip
to hold plastic
in place   Frame
                Flat

Wood strip
to hold plastic
in place

Flat

Film
stretched
directly on
flat or flat
put in large
polyethylene bag

42. Cover the seed flat with polyethylene until the seeds germinate (Photo courtesy U. S. Department of Agriculture)

43. To transplant seedlings to a larger container, the seedlings should be lifted gently with a knife blade (Photo courtesy U. S. Department of Agriculture)

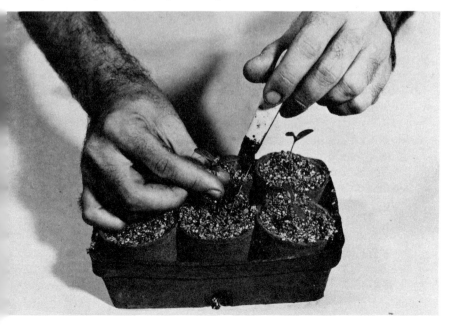

put the container in an area where it will receive light and be protected from low temperatures.

Transplanting

When the plants have developed two true leaves, they are ready to transplant to another container to give them more room to develop. Each seedling should be lifted gently, with care, with a knife blade (Figure 43) and moved. Keep handling of plants to a minimum.

Setting Out

When frost damage is past, garden planting can begin. Assuming the beds and planting areas are ready to receive plants, the containers can be brought out and kept in a shaded spot while planting goes on. We personally like to plant in the late afternoon to give the transplants a chance to recover during a period of lower night temperatures and darkness. When planting is finished, soak the beds with as fine a sprinkle as possible. The next day check around the base of each plant and fill any low spots that may have resulted from the watering.

VEGETATIVE PROPAGATION

There are four methods of vegetative propagation that can be used to increase plant numbers. Not all plants can be increased vegetatively by the same methods.

The methods are cuttings, division, layering, and grafting. The last method will be covered in a separate chapter.

Successful propagating will depend on selection of vigorous and healthy parent plants, carrying on the operation at the correct time of the year, protecting the propagating material from drying, and concerned care for the new plants until they are successfully established.

All of these vegetative methods give the gardener the opportunity of reproducing a plant with all the characteristics of the mother plant.

CUTTING

The most widely used method of producing like offspring from a parent plant is by cuttings, which can be made from roots, stems,

44. Moisten the cutting and dip the cut end in the rooting hormone powder (Photo courtesy U. S. Department of Agriculture)

and leaves. The greatest success will be had by using stem cuttings, because roots develop more readily than do stems. Leaf cuttings are used infrequently, most often with African violets.

Cuttings are divided into two major classes, hardwood or dormant season, and softwood or growing season. All cuttings should be made longer than the final length required, and trimmed before bundling. Always use a sharp cutting tool to take cuttings and for trimming, and be sure the cuttings are planted upright.

Rooting Medium

The number of rooting media used to propagate cuttings approximate the number of people who root cuttings. The basic requirements are water- and oxygen-holding capacity, the ability to support cuttings upright, and freedom from insects and diseases.

Peat moss, sand, vermiculite, perlite, cinders, and soil in a variety of ratios are the basic materials used.

Rooting cuttings in water is not recommended, although we have used this method in propagating aucuba, because it often results in tender, fragile roots.

Rooting Hormones

Rooting hormones are available which hasten and encourage root formation in leafy stem cuttings but are not overly successful with hardwood cuttings.

These compounds usually are based on synthetic chemicals and include indole acetic acid, indole butyric acid, and naphthalene acetic, singly and sometimes combined.

Two simple methods of using hormones are suggested. In one, the base of the cutting, slanted at a 45-degree angle, is dipped in water, and the excess water shaken off, then the bottom inch is dipped into the hormone powder (Figure 44), the excess shaken off, and the cuttings then set in a moist medium in a plastic bag or in a seed flat or bed (Figure 42), covered with plastic to maintain a high humidity.

The second method uses a water solution of a growth hormone in which the cuttings are soaked for two to three hours, and then planted as described above.

When treatment is complete, place the cuttings into prepared holes, made with a pencil, to a depth of 2 inches. Then firm the medium around the cutting and water.

High humidity, adequate light, and a temperature between 65° F. and 85° F. are required.

Time to Root Cuttings

The condition of a plant is as good an indication of the correct time to make cuttings as is the time of year. Healthy, vigorous plants with dark green leaves are best.

Easily rooted cuttings can be propagated at any time of the year. Chrysanthemum, geranium, forsythia, and others are in this category. Other plants are more specific and are best rooted at a specific time. (See Table 2 at the end of this chapter.)

Azaleas and rhododendrons can be propagated by softwood cuttings after flowering or as semi-hardwood cuttings in September.

Narrow-leaved evergreens, mentioned elsewhere, do best if the cuttings are taken after one or two frosts, or after a month or more of low winter temperatures.

Other times to root cuttings are given in Table 2.

Hardwood cuttings, or dormant cuttings, are made from dormant material, after foliage has fallen off on deciduous plants. Evergreen cuttings would, of course, still have their leaves.

45. Hardwood cuttings are placed upside down in moist sand, and covered to a depth of 4 to 6 inches (Photo courtesy U. S. Department of Agriculture)

The cuttings can be bundled as 6- to 8-inch pieces and stored upside down in moist sand, covered to a depth of 4 to 6 inches, outdoors in a well-drained spot (Figure 45).

In the spring the cuttings can be set out in the position chosen for them in the garden, or in a second-stage area such as a cold frame. The cuttings should be set deep enough to leave just the top bud exposed.

Leafy stem cuttings are made during the growing season and include leaves or needles. Those made from herbaceous plants should be 4 to 5 inches long and from woody plants 6 to 9 inches long. The leaves on the lower half of these cuttings are stripped to reduce water loss. To protect the cuttings from excess water loss before planting, they can be put in polyethylene bags, in shade (Figure 46).

The cuttings should be treated with hormones, inserted into the rooting medium 1 to 2 inches in a hole made previously with a pencil, watered, and the soil packed firmly around the base. Mulch may be used to good advantage.

While the cuttings are being readied for planting the bases should be kept in water, in a shady spot. If a delay in planting is inevitable the cuttings can be stored in the refrigerator, wrapped in damp toweling, in a plastic bag.

The steps required to propagate leafy, softwood cuttings in the home in a windowsill "greenhouse" are demonstrated in the illustrations (Figures 47 to 54) in this chapter. A goodly number of such cuttings can be forced if you have a large enough number of windowsills.

The out-planting procedure should follow the same steps given for hardwood cuttings.

Newly set-out cuttings, hardwood or softwood, can be protected from excess water loss by placing a jar over them.

Root cuttings are more of a challenge than are stem cuttings, as they must produce stems, more difficult than growing new roots. However, woody plants that sucker can be propagated by selecting roots the thickness of a pencil and making cuttings 3 to 4 inches long in the fall or winter. The cuttings are planted either horizontally or with the thicker, stem end at the top.

After the first growing season these plants are ready for the garden.

An earlier start can be had by starting the cuttings indoors and transplanting to the garden in the spring.

Leaf cuttings. Not widely used, this technique is suited for certain thick-leaved herbaceous plants.

A rooting media, such as described elsewhere in this chapter, is required, and a suitable container.

To make leaf cuttings of African violets and gloxinia, select healthy mature leaves and remove them from the mother plant with

46. Cuttings can be placed in a polyethylene bag with soil mixture to protect against excess water loss (Photo courtesy U. S. Department of Agriculture)

½ to 1 inch of leafstalk. Insert the leafstalk into the medium so that the leaf blade is above the surface of the medium. New roots will develop in three to four weeks and new shoots in another three to four weeks.

Fibrous rooted begonias are propagated in a slightly different manner. The leaves chosen are removed and the main veins of the leaf blade are cut in six to eight places. The leaf is then anchored firmly in the medium. Toothpicks around the edges are useful. New plants will develop at the cut places.

Covering these leaves with jars or glasses is recommended to maintain humidity.

LAYERING

Layering is a method of vegetative propagation which stimulates the growth of roots on a stem of a woody plant while still attached to the mother plant. With this technique the mother plant nourishes its offspring until it is ready for removal.

47. The first step in constructing your greenhouse is to sift peat moss through quarter-inch wire mesh (Photo courtesy U. S. Department of Agriculture)

48. Step 2. Combine two parts of the screened peat moss with one part sand, mix well (Photo courtesy U. S. Department of Agriculture)

Air layering, also called Chinese layering, is a popular method of propagating many woody shrubs and trees, indoors and outdoors.

A one-year-old branch or stem is easy to work with and is recommended, as it roots readily. Select an area 12 to 18 inches from the tip of the branch, and remove leaves 4 to 6 inches on either side of the spot where you plan on the roots originating.

With a sharp knife make a diagonal upward cut 1 to 2 inches long on the limb, ending on the upper center. Wedge the cut open with a small twig and dust the wound with one of the rooting hormones.

Place a handful of moist sphagnum moss around and between the cut surfaces (Figure 55) and tie tightly with string, a heavy rubber band, or raffia. Next wrap polyethylene tightly around the sphagnum moss (Figure 56), with ends of the plastic folded and fastened firmly to the limb with waterproof tape. A well-done job will keep the sphagnum moss moist a year. If necessary, arrange shade for the layering area. Among the plants propagated by this method are croton, dracaena, and rubber plants, to name a very few.

Tip layering. This method is useful with forsythia, although we find our own plants tip-layer without help. The formal technique calls for placing the scraped tip of a shoot into 1 to 2 inches of soil. The tip should be held in place with a weight.

Mound layering, or stooling, is useful with hydrangea, some spiraea, quince, gooseberry, all of which root in one year, and magnolia and rhododendron, which require two years.

During the dormant season the plants should be pruned back heavily, a few inches above soil level. In the spring when growth begins, the bases are covered with soil, leaving the growing points uncovered. Soil is mounded over the base of the plant during the growing season until it is 6 to 8 inches deep. One-year stems layered in the spring will be rooted in the fall and can be cut off and stored over winter, or planted. Two-year plants will require two growing seasons.

Simple layering requires a low-growing branch to be bent to the ground before growth begins in the spring. Twelve inches from the branch tip a notch may be cut in the bottom of the stem, or the area wounded by scraping with the back of a knife; a slanting 2-inch cut

49. Step 3. Moisten the peat moss and sand with as much water as the mixture can absorb without being too wet (Photo courtesy U. S. Department of Agriculture)

on the upper side of the wounded spot is sometimes used. Root hormones can be applied to the cut areas, and the tip bent upright. Pin the branch into the soil between the cut area and the trunk. Next a peg of some sort should be placed directly over the cut area and the pegged branch covered with 3 to 4 inches of rich soil. The soil should be heaped around the upturned stem so the cut is 3 to 5 inches underground. Pack the soil firmly and keep moist.

Spring layered branches will be ready for a nursery area the following spring, fall layered branches the second spring. After the offspring is cut from the mother plant, it should remain in place three to four weeks.

Division is a rather simple method of cutting a parent plant into two or more plants, by careful use of a sharp knife or spade.

Perennials should be moved and divided every three to four years.

50. Step 4. The cuttings chosen should be light green in color, which would make them the current season's growth (Photo courtesy U. S. Department of Agriculture)

Soil fertility becomes depleted, growth and flowering are reduced by crowding (Figure 57).

For best results the side shoots are transplanted, and the center of the clump is discarded. Fall is the best time for this operation in the Carolinas.

Clumps for transplanting should have three to five shoots. Less will provide an inadequate floral display. When replanting do not over-crowd the area. Surplus plants can be planted elsewhere or given away.

51. Step 5. The cuttings should snap when broken, should not be soft and rubbery (Photo courtesy U. S. Department of Agriculture)

Figure 57 shows the steps involved in dividing perennials.

Plants propagating by rhizome, such as iris, should be divided no later than at five-year intervals. In some cases a shorter time may be desirable, if growth is somewhat dense.

Iris can be divided in the late summer or early fall after blooming is finished. Cut the leaves to one third of their height, then dig up the entire clump of rhizomes. Soil should then be washed away, division made (Figure 58), and the rhizomes, each with a visible growing point and some roots, planted immediately.

Dividing tubers such as peonies differ in minor details as shown in Figure 59. A clump is dug up carefully, the soil washed away, diseased and decayed tubers removed, and the clump separated into pieces each with three to five eyes, using a clean knife. Each tuber should have a tap root. Replant immediately.

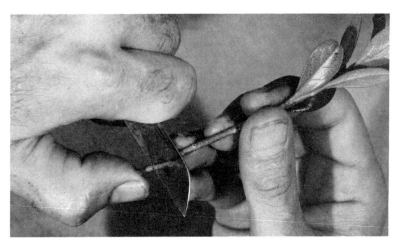

52. Step 6. The cuttings should be 4 to 6 inches long with the leaves removed on the lower third. Cut the end of the cuttings diagonally and dip in rooting hormone. (Photo courtesy U. S. Department of Agriculture)

53. Step 7. The cuttings should be placed in a plastic bag with the moistened soil mixture, and sprinkled with a little water. Then seal the bag with a rubber band. (Photo courtesy U. S. Department of Agriculture)

54. Step 8. Place the bag in a northern window where it receives plenty of light but no direct sun (Photo courtesy U. S. Department of Agriculture)

55. Air layering. Place a handful of moist peat moss around and between the cut surfaces of the branch. Tie tightly with string. (Photo courtesy U. S. Department of Agriculture)

56. Wrap polyethylene around the peat moss, fold the ends of the plastic in, and fasten to the limb with waterproof tape (Photo courtesy U. S. Department of Agriculture)

When— **How—**

Flowers are small

Stems fall over easily (have little vigor)

Root has many underdeveloped shoots

Root center is hollow and dead

Bottom foliage is scant and poor

Lift plant.   Wash most of soil from root system.   Select divisions.

Pull or cut apart separate divisions. Each division contains old stem, vegetative lateral shoot, and root system.

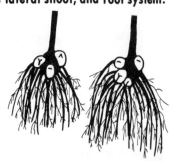

Old stems from previous season

Root center is hollow and dead

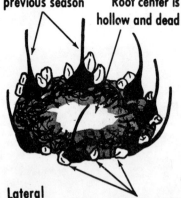

Lateral vegetative shoots are pale green or almost white when they start to develop

Plant divisions that have several vegetative lateral shoots and vigorous root systems.

Discard these or plant several together.

57. The steps involved in separating perennials for replanting
(Photo courtesy U. S. Department of Agriculture)

Left, small rhizome divisions; right, large rhizome divisions.

58. Dividing a rhizome for replanting (Photo courtesy U. S. Department of Agriculture)

59. Dividing a tuber for replanting (Photo courtesy U. S. Department of Agriculture)

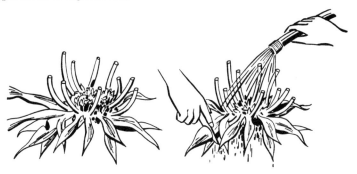

1. The tubers on established plants look like a collection of fat sweetpotatoes.

2. Wash away all soil and cut away any damaged parts.

3. Cut clump apart so each piece will have three to five eyes and strong tubers.

4. Shorten tubers to 4- to 6-inch stubs.

TABLE 2 *Some suggested times to propagate stem cuttings of various plants*[1]

PLANT	SEASON
abelia	late summer through early fall
althaea	early summer
American holly	late summer through early fall
arborvitae	late summer through winter
azalea	spring through fall
barberry	early summer to early fall
beauty bush	early summer
boxwood	early summer through fall
butterfly bush	early summer through early fall
camellia	later summer through fall
clematis	early summer
cotoneaster	early summer
deutzia	early summer
dogwood	during spring blooming
elaeagnus	late summer through fall
flowering almond	early summer
forsythia	late summer through early fall
gardenia	late summer through early fall
Japanese magnolia	midsummer
jasmine	midsummer
juniper	late summer through early fall
mock orange	midsummer
mountain laurel	late summer through early winter
pyracantha	late summer through early fall
rhododendron	late fall through winter
rose	late summer through fall
spiraea	later summer through early fall
viburnum	later summer through early fall
weigela	late summer through fall
wisteria	early summer

[1] Based on North Carolina State University Horticultural Information Leaflet No. 429.

RECOMMENDED REFERENCES

North Carolina Agricultural Extension Service, *Intermittent Mist Propagation.* Circular 506, North Carolina State University, Raleigh, N.C. 27607, June 1969.

————, *Propagation of Trees and Shrubs.* Horticultural Leaflet No. 111, North Carolina State University, Raleigh, N.C. 27607, November 1965.

————, *Proper Time to Root Cuttings.* Horticultural Information Leaflet No. 420, North Carolina State University, Raleigh, N.C. 27607.

————, *Transplanting Table for Some Herbaceous Perennials.* Horticultural Information Leaflet No. 510, North Carolina State University, Raleigh, N.C. 27607, November 1965.

————, *Transplanting Trees and Shrubs.* Horticultural Information Leaflet No. 401, North Carolina State University, Raleigh, N.C. 27607, October 1965.

U. S. Department of Agriculture, *Greenhouses Framing for Plastic Covering.* Miscellaneous Publication No. 1114, Washington, D.C. 20250.

————, *Home Propagation of Ornamental Trees and Shrubs.* Home and Garden Bulletin No. 80, Washington, D.C. 20250, October 1967.

————, *Lath House for Nursery Plants.* Miscellaneous Publication No. 1154, Washington, D.C. 20250, December 1969.

————, *Mini-Hotbed and Propagating Frame.* Miscellaneous Publication No. 1184, Washington, D.C. 20250, December 1970.

————, *Plastic Covered Greenhouse Frame.* Miscellaneous Publication No. 1111, Washington, D.C. 20250, January 1969.

————, *Propagation Unit for Plants.* Miscellaneous Publication No. 1215, Washington, D.C. 20250, December 1965.

————, *Sphagnum Moss for Plant Propagation.* Farmers Bulletin No. 2085, Washington, D.C. 20250, July 1955.

————, *Transplanting Ornamental Trees and Shrubs.* Home and Garden Bulletin No. 192, Washington, D.C. 20250, March 1972.

CHAPTER 9

Budding and Grafting

Budding and grafting are two additional means of vegetative propagation. However, these methods use a basically different procedure than the methods discussed in the previous chapter.

In propagation by layering and cutting we create a totally new and complete plant exactly like its parent, and originating from a single parent. With budding and grafting we change the flowering, growth, or fruiting habits of a plant and produce a new plant with rootstock characteristics of one plant and flowering, fruiting, or growth characteristics of another plant.

The methods discussed in this chapter are used if propagation by cuttings is difficult, or if only a few buds of a desired plant are available. If flowering or fruiting properties of a plant are desirable, but its own roots are not adapted to a particular soil type or drainage problem, or to an insect or disease problem, a rootstock meeting the requirements can be used in combination with grafting and budding to build a desirable plant. Some rootstocks have a dwarfing effect, and are often used to produce a smaller back-yard specimen. Table 3 at the end of this chapter lists the most used ornamentals of the Carolinas and gives information as to the kind of budding and grafting used, as well as the best time for each plant and method.

BUDDING

Budding is best done in the fall for most, but not all, plants. This allows time for a sound union to form before spring growth begins. The major time determinant is the ease with which the bark separates from the wood, allowing space for the bud to be inserted. The principal need in successful budding is to establish contact of the cambium layers, the cells whose role is growth and development of new cells. The cambium occurs below the bark.

Shield Budding

Shield budding, and several variations, is the most widely used technique.

The stock into which buds are inserted should be at least as thick as a pencil, or slightly larger, whether on a young nursery tree or shrub, or stock to be planted. The buds should be plump and healthy and dormant, free of insect and disease symptoms.

Now start a cut just below the bud to be used, just enough to get a thin sliver of wood with a shield of bark (Figure 60, A) about ¾ of an inch long.

Using a sharp knife, a 1-inch-long vertical cut is made on the stock from bottom to top, 3 to 4 inches from the bottom, carefully, so that only the bark is cut. The top of the T should be made the same way, going one third the way around the stock (B).

With the knife point carefully lift the bark along both sides of the vertical cut (C).

Then insert the lower part of the shield with its bud into the T (D). Last, using raffia or a rubber band, bind the bud in place (E) above and below, but without covering the bud.

About a month later carefully cut the raffia away, at which time the union of bud and stock should be complete. In the spring, at bud-swell, cut the stock plant about an inch above the bud to force the bud to grow.

Plate Budding

Plate budding resembles shield budding with a few minor differences. A piece of bark and wood is cut off the stock and a bud is placed against the cut area of the stock and bound in place with waxed cloth (Figure 61).

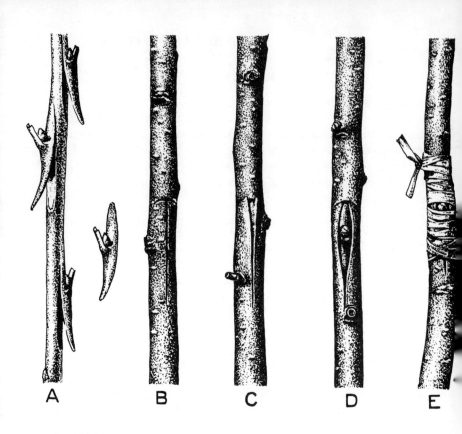

A   B   C   D   E

60. Shield budding (Photo courtesy U. S. Department of Agriculture)

GRAFTING

Grafting provides a means for working with large trees and shrubs. As with budding, grafting permits the desired qualities of rootstock and top to be joined to produce a plant with specified qualities and characteristics. This method is very much quicker than breeding a plant with certain required qualities.

The two parts used in grafting are the scion, which is the transferred part, and the rootstock. The two parts must be botanically closely related, usually of the same genus and species, although it is possible to graft plants of the same genus but different species. Apples are grafted onto apples, dogwood onto dogwood, and roses onto roses. In each case different varieties are used, but all of the same species. Quince rootstock has been used to dwarf pears, apricot to

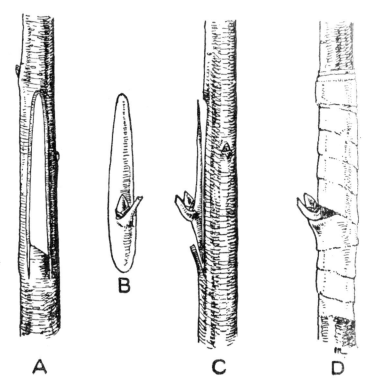

A simple and useful form of plate bud. A, Stock prepared by paring off a piece of bark, exposing the wood; B, bud cut similar to that for ordinary shield budding; C, bud in place; D, completed operation. Bud wrapped with waxed muslin

61. Plate budding (Courtesy U. S. Department of Agriculture)

dwarf peaches; and Russian scientists have grafted tomato tops onto potato roots, plants in the same family.

Both stock and scion must be healthy, vigorous, and free of disease and insects. The key to successful grafting is a close fit of the scion and stock at the cambium layer.

Either fall or spring is a suitable time for grafting.

Whip Grafting

Whip grafting is adapted to use with small plant parts. The scion material, about 1 foot in length and the thickness of a pencil, is collected during the dormant season. Year-old shoots or water sprouts are ideal. However, be sure that sprouts cut from the bottom of the

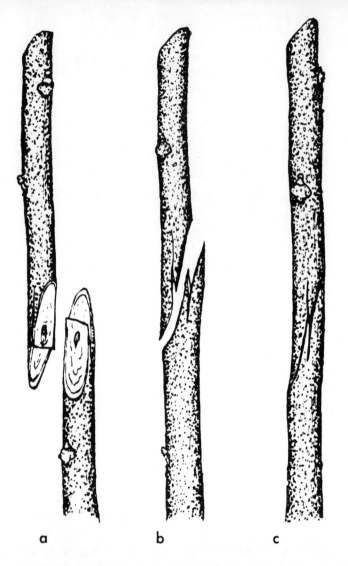

a   b   c

62. Whip grafting (Courtesy North Carolina State University)

plant do not originate from belowground. Such material may be of rootstock origin and not at all what is wanted.

The scion wood can be stored in a plastic bag in a refrigerator, or in a box of damp sawdust in a cool spot, such as a basement, until needed.

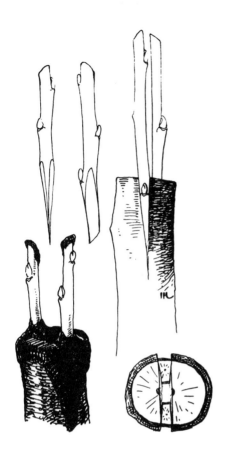

63. Cleft grafting (Photo courtesy U. S. Department of Agriculture)

The scion can be grafted to a young plant in the nursery row, or to a cutting made of the main root of a seedling. If root cuttings are used they should be about 6 inches long. The thickness of both rootstock and scion should match as close as possible. The scion should have about three buds.

Sloping cuts are made on stock and scion, 1½ inches long. Then cuts about ¾ of an inch long are made in stock and scion and lastly the two parts are fitted together (Figure 62) so that the cambiums touch on at least one side. The point of union is then bound firmly with cotton dipped in grafting wax, or with grafting bands.

The grafts can be tied in bundles of six to twelve and stored in damp sand or peat moss, in a container in a cool, shady spot. In the spring, after last frost, the grafts are planted about a foot apart, in a nursery row, with the graft union just below the soil surface. Keep clean of weeds, and water as needed.

Cleft Grafting (Figure 63)

This technique is used to change some characteristics of flowers, foliage, or fruit of a large established plant. It is carried out during the dormant season, in late winter, on a day when the temperature is comfortable enough to work outdoors.

The scion wood is selected from the previous year's growth; two or three varieties can be used to create an unusual effect of flowering, foliage, or fruit.

The scions each should have three good buds, with the cut made about an inch below the bottom bud.

The stock is prepared by sawing straight across where you wish to make the graft. This can be the main trunk, or a large limb. A metal wedge or chisel is driven into the trunk 2 to 3 inches, and the cut wedged open.

The scions are trimmed with a sharp knife to form a wedge. The cuts are begun just below the bottom bud. The scions are then fitted into the wedged stock at a slight angle toward the outside of the stock to increase chances of cambium contact.

When the scions are in place, carefully remove the wedge so that the scions are held firmly by the stock. Then coat all exposed surfaces with grafting wax or tree-coating compound and cover with a plastic refrigerator bag tied around the stock. Shade the site of the graft. In the spring after growth begins, remove the plastic bag and recoat the cut surfaces. At the end of the first growing season cut off the slower-growing scion of the two and coat again to reduce insect and disease attacks.

Saddle grafting (Figure 64) is used with rhododendrons and lilacs, and is relatively simple. A V cleft is made in the stock and a wedge in the scion, which are then joined together for maximum cambium contact tied tightly together with grafting bands or cotton dipped in grafting wax. The entire site is then coated with tree compound or wax.

Veneer grafting (Figure 65) is used for narrow leaf evergreen propagation. Very similar to side grafting, it differs only in the shorter wedge of the scion.

Side grafting is frequently used with junipers, as well as other

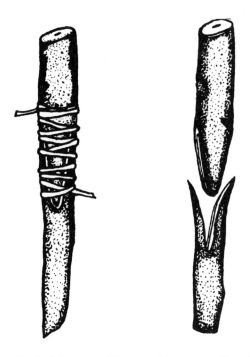

64. Saddle graft (Courtesy North Carolina State University)

65. Veneer graft (Courtesy North Carolina State University)

plants. A long strip of bark is cut from the stick, about 2 inches long, and a one-sided wedge to match the stock is placed in position and bound firmly in place and waxed. A variation of this method requires a long, sloping cut 2 inches long made in the stock and a pointed wedge to match inserted in the stock. The two parts are bound firmly and then waxed (Figure 66).

Bark grafts are useful for outdoor work when the stock is larger than the scion. The stocks are made with one side of the wedge longer than the other. The stock is prepared by removing a strip of bark and the longer side of the scion wedge is placed against the stock. The stock and scion are fastened firmly in place and carefully waxed.

66. Side graft (Courtesy North Carolina State University)

TABLE 3 *Methods and time of budding and grafting recommended for ornamentals in the Carolinas*[1]

PLANT	GRAFT OR BUD	TIME
amelanchier	veneer, side	winter
	bud	summer
ash	side	spring
azalea 'Indica'	veneer	summer
beech	side	winter, spring
birch	veneer, side	winter
	bud	summer
camellia	cleft, side	spring[2]
catalpa	whip	spring
cedar	veneer	winter
Chamaecyparis (false cypress)	veneer, side	winter, spring
chestnut	whip, side	winter
chionanthus (fringe tree)	side	spring
clematis	whip	winter
corylus (filbert)	veneer	winter
cotoneaster	side	winter
crab apple	bud	summer
deodar cedar	veneer, side	August, September
dogwood	whip, side	winter, spring
	bud	summer
elaeagnus	veneer, side	winter, spring
elm	whip	winter
	bud	summer
euonymus	whip, saddle, side	winter
exochorda (pearl bush)	whip	summer
fir	veneer, side	winter

[1] Adapted from Extension Circular No. 326, 1972, N. C. Agricultural Extension Service, North Carolina State University, Raleigh.
[2] Protection required.

PLANT	GRAFT OR BUD	TIME
hawthorn	veneer, whip	winter
	bud	summer
hickory	veneer, whip	winter, spring
		summer
honeylocust	veneer	winter
hydrangea	cleft, whip	spring
juniper	veneer	January
laburnum	side	spring
larch	whip, cleft, veneer	winter, spring
lilac	whip, saddle	spring
	bud	summer
locust	veneer	spring
magnolia	side, veneer	summer
	bud	summer
maple	veneer, side	winter
mountain ash	side	spring
	bud	summer
oak	veneer	winter, spring
Oregon grape (mahonia)	side, cleft	spring
persimmon	veneer	winter
	bud	summer
pine	veneer, side	March to August
poplar	whip	spring
Prunus (plum, cherry, peach)	bud	summer
redbud	side	spring
rhododendron	side	winter
		summer (June, July, August)
rose	bud	winter, spring
spruce	veneer	January
tuliptree	side	winter
	bud	summer
tupelo tree	side	spring

PLANT	GRAFT OR BUD	TIME
viburnum	side, cleft	spring
	bud	summer
walnut	side	spring
	bud	spring
weigela	whip	spring
willow	side	spring
wisteria	veneer, side	winter, spring

RECOMMENDED REFERENCES

North Carolina Agricultural Extension Service, *Fruit Trees and Ornamentals: Budding and Grafting.* Extension Circular No. 326, North Carolina State University, Raleigh, N.C. 27607, April 1972.

CHAPTER 10

Perennials

A perennial is a herbaceous plant which lives for several years. In gardens these plants are usually grown for their foliage or flowers, or both. Some have tops which are perennial, others have tops which die during winter. In this group we exclude trees, shrubs, and bulbs. Perennials have a built-in advantage over annuals because they do not have to be replanted each year.

A perennial border around the family area can be a pleasant sight from inside the home as well as serving to mark off the area. A perennial foundation planting can bring together the landscape and the home in a unified format.

Perennials should have a "frame" or background to accent their foliage and flowering qualities. The home can serve this function, as can evergreen trees and shrubs.

With planning, a program of perennial planting can be established to provide color at times when the garden might otherwise be relatively colorless.

The first step in establishing a perennial border is to prepare a pencil design on graph paper with a scale of one unit to 5 feet, to show the location of plants as well as the shape and area of the border.

Three questions should be answered in planning.

(*1*) Have plants been selected which will carry out your design and goals? Plants do grow, vertically as well as horizontally.

(*2*) Are these plants suited to your region, and to your particular growing conditions?

(*3*) Are the plants available at nearby nurseries?

Plants can be selected with a number of goals in mind. Some growers might want a continuous bloom of color during the growing season, some might like plants with different foliage textures as well as variations in forms. The choice of perennials to provide a display of color to a great extent depends on personal preferences. We feel that if you like it and find it pleasant, then it is desirable.

Form

Form may be based on single plants, as well as the sum of form of several plants added together.

Some plants create a feeling of "upness," such as hollyhock, foxglove, and delphinium. Other plants can create an image of horizontal flowing movement; for example, peony, phlox, and sweet william.

Usually "horizontal" plants predominate in perennial plantings, with an occasional vertical plant to create interest and break up the sameness of all horizontal forms.

Texture

Texture is a composite of leaves and branches. Shape and size of leaves, bark texture, and branch color as well as branch density and arrangement are important to texture. Plants with large leaves should not be interplanted with finely branched plants.

Soil Preparation

Because these plants occupy the area for several years, soil preparation and soil quality are important.

The beds should be prepared to at least a depth of 18 inches, and compost or other available materials should be incorporated into the soil before planting.

Drainage

Poor drainage can result in poor growth, and in extreme cases, death of the plants. Good surface drainage to move water away from borders is essential. In low areas it may be necessary to dig out the border area to a depth of 2 feet and lay down a 6-inch layer of coarse gravel, followed by a 2-inch layer of coarse sand, topped with soil mixed with organic materials. In Chapter 12 a simple drainage test is described.

Fertilizing

If soil tests show a need for fertilizer it should be added to the border area and worked into the soil.

As perennials develop, fertilizer should be added once or twice a year, in the spring as growth begins, and possibly a second time halfway through the growing season.

Cultivation

Weed control is of major importance and the best way to do it is with a hoe, supplemented with hand weeding as required. The amount of weeding required will be less as the plants grow and produce more shade, reducing weed growth.

Watering

Depending on soil type, 1 to 2 inches of water a week will be enough, with watering done in the morning preferably, to allow the foliage to dry out. High moisture can result in an increase in leaf fungus diseases.

Staking

Some perennials, because they are top-heavy, require staking. Bent or broken stems cannot transport water effectively to the plant tops, and broken areas provide entrances for disease organisms. Stakes help keep the plants erect and help protect against wind damage. The stakes are pushed deep enough in the ground to hold steady.

Staking should be done when the plants are set out. The stakes can be bought in garden stores in different lengths or can be made of available materials, such as dowels, bamboo, or wire. Most are reusable for several seasons.

Use wire covered with plastic, similar to the closures used for freezer and sandwich bags, to tie the plant to the stake. Do not use string as it decays and looks straggly. Be sure to use a double loop

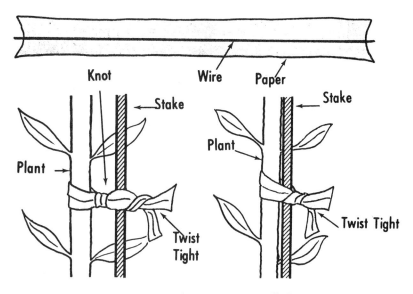

67. Proper staking of perennial (Photo courtesy U. S. Department of Agriculture)

(Figure 67) with one loop around the plant stem and the other loop around the stake. A single loop for stem and stake will result in the plant's drooping.

PLANTS

Achillea millefolium, yarrow

Yarrow grows in all regions to 2 feet in height and blooms from June to September, with pink, gold, or white flowers. It is adapted to most any soil including poor, dry soil, in sun. Because it is somewhat drought-resistant, it is excellent for hot, dry places. The seeds germinate in one to two weeks and can be planted in early spring or late fall, the plants set out about 3 feet apart. Water with a mist or through burlap until germination takes place. Used also as a ground cover and in borders. Clumps may be divided and replanted.

Althaea rosea, hollyhock

Hollyhock grows in all regions to 6 feet in height with flowers from June to first frost in a wide range of colors and many blossoms on each flower stalk. Although it prefers a deep, well-drained soil high in humus, in sun, it will grow in poorer soils. The seeds, which germinate in ten days, can be planted from spring to early September.

Plants should be set out 3 feet apart. Used as a border and to screen areas, and as a backdrop for smaller plants.

Alyssum saxatile, 'Compacta,' basket of gold, hardy alyssum

Hardy alyssum grows in all regions, to 1 foot in height, with yellow flowers in early spring. It grows in dry, sandy soil on fairly fertile, well-drained soil in sun. The seeds which germinate in three to four weeks may be planted in early spring or in August to September and wintered over. Plant distance is 2 feet apart. The double-flower varieties can only be grown by dividing the clumps. Used in rock gardens, for cut flowers, and edging.

Anchusa italica, A. myosotidiflora, A. azurea, alkanet

Alkanet grows in all regions from 3 to 5 feet in height, with blue flowers June to July. It needs a fairly rich, well-drained soil, and is adapted to sun or partial shade. At lower elevations it is best to plant in the partial shade or cooler spots. The seeds, refrigerated for three days before planting, can be sown all during the growing season, and germinate in three to four weeks. The roots may be divided and replanted. Plants should be set 2 feet apart. It reseeds itself and may form new plants if left alone. Alkanet needs frequent watering during dry periods. Staking during flowering may be needed for taller plants. Used for borders, backgrounds, and cut flowers.

Anthemis tinctoria, camomile, golden daisy

Camomile grows in all regions, to 2 feet in height, with yellow flowers from June to first frost. It grows in dry, sandy, poor soils in sun. The seeds, which germinate in three to four weeks, can be started indoors about two months before setting out. Plants should be set out 2 feet apart. Used in borders.

Aquilegia canadensis, columbine

Columbine grows in all regions to 1½ feet in height, with red and yellow flowers appearing from April to June. It grows in full sun but will tolerate medium to heavy shade, and prefers a well-drained, loamy soil. The seeds, which germinate in about four weeks, can be planted during the growing season. Plants bloom the second year. Plants should be set 1 to 1½ feet apart. Older plants can be divided in August or September. Used in rock gardens and borders.

Arabis spp., rock cress

Rock cress grows in all regions to 1 foot in height, bearing white fragrant flowers in early spring. Single and double varieties are available. Cutting off the flowers as they dry encourages new flowers. It is fairly drought-resistant and grows in well-drained soil or rocky areas and is adapted to dry to medium moist places in sun or partial shade. The seeds, which germinate in a week, can be planted during the growing season. The plants may also be divided and replanted. Plants should be set 1 foot apart. Used for cut flowers, as an edging plant, and in rock gardens.

Armeria alpina, sea pink

This armeria grows in all regions to 2 feet in height, with white and pink flowers that appear in May and June. It does best in dry, sandy soil. The seeds, which germinate in about ten days, can be planted in a shaded seedbed during the growing season. Plants should be set 1 foot apart. Used for borders, rock gardens, and edging.

Artemisia stelleriana, dusty miller, southernwood, wormwood

This plant grows in all regions to 2½ feet in height and is known for its silvery-white or dusty leaves. It may not bloom the first year. Flowers are small yellow or white. It does well in any ordinary soil or even dry poor soil, in full sun or partial shade. The seed can be planted from late spring to late summer and plants should be set 1 foot apart. Because it is resistant to salt spray it does well along the ocean. Used for edging, as a specimen in front of evergreens, and borders.

Aster alpinus, aster

The aster grows in all regions, from 1 to 5 feet in height, and blooms in June. It grows in sun or shade. The seeds germinate in two to three weeks and can be planted in early spring. The plants can also be divided and replanted 3 feet apart. Used for cut flowers, borders, and rock gardens.

Astilbe spp., astilbe

Astible is adapted to the Appalachian mountains and the Piedmont plateau and grows to 2 feet in height, with light, feathery flowers borne on spikes in July to August. It prefers loamy, moist soil with partial shade. The seeds, which germinate in two to three weeks, can be planted in early spring. The plants can also be divided and replanted in the spring. Set plants 2 feet apart. Used in borders.

Bellis perennis, English daisy

This plant occurs in all regions, grows to 6 inches in height, and blooms during the growing season. It requires well-drained, moist soil and partial shade. The seeds germinate in about a week and plants should be set 6 inches apart. Used for ground cover and in masses.

Campanula spp., bellflower, Canterbury bell

Campanula grows in all regions to 2 to 3 feet in height with bell-shaped blue or white flowers. It prefers a well-drained, fertile soil and most varieties prefer full sunlight; *C. medium* prefers partial shade. The seeds, which germinate in about three weeks, can be planted during the growing season. The plants may be divided every other year and replanted. Set plants 1½ feet apart. Used in rock gardens and at the edge of borders.

Centaurea montana, centaurea, coneflower

Centaurea grows in all regions to 2 feet in height with blue, rose, or white flowers from May to September. Any good garden soil in sun is suitable. The seeds, which germinate in three to four weeks, can be planted in early spring. The plants may also be divided and replanted since they spread easily by underground stems. Set plants 1 foot apart. To encourage longer blooming remove flowers as they dry. Used for cut flowers and borders.

Cerastium tomentosum, snow-in-summer

This silvery-foliaged plant, found in all regions, grows to 6 inches in height, with white five-petaled flowers April to June. It does well in dry, sunny locations in any good soil. The seeds, which germinate in three weeks, can be planted in early spring. The plants may also be divided and replanted very early in the summer. Set plants 1½ feet apart. Used as ground cover and in rock gardens.

Chrysanthemum hortorum, hardy mum, hardy chrysanthemum

These fall bloomers thrive in all regions, growing to 2 feet in height, and are available as single and double varieties, in many colors. They prefer full sun and a well-drained, loamy soil. They are propagated by dividing older plants or from rooted cuttings. Early in the season the tops are pinched back to encourage low, compact growth. Used for cut flowers and borders.

Chrysanthemum maximum, Shasta daisy

The Shasta daisy is adapted to all regions and grows to 2 feet in height. This daisy is larger than the common daisy, and blooms in midsummer. It will grow on a range of soils from sandy soil to heavy clay, but prefers a well-drained, deep soil high in humus, in full sun. It may be grown by dividing the plants and replanting in the spring or by taking stem cuttings. The seeds, which germinate in a week, can be planted from early spring to September. Plants should be spaced 2½ feet apart. It needs winter protection. Used for cut flowers and borders.

Coreopsis grandiflora, coreopsis

Adapted to all regions, coreopsis grows to 3 feet in height with yellow flowers appearing from June to early frost. It is available in single and double forms. It will grow on light loam as well as rich soil in full sun. It is drought-resistant. The seeds, which germinate in a week, can be planted all during the growing season. If sown early in the spring they may bloom the first year. The plants may also be divided and replanted. Set plants 2½ feet apart. Used in borders.

Delphinium spp., larkspur

Larkspur grows best in the Appalachian mountains and the Piedmont plateau, from 1½ to 4 feet in height. Warm-climate varieties should be chosen, which will bloom from June to late summer if old flowers are removed. Flower colors range from blue to purple and gray. Well-drained, sunny locations are best. The seeds, which germinate in about three weeks, can be planted all during the growing season. Cuttings may be taken in the summer if desired. They usually do not bloom the first year. If started indoors earlier they should be put in peat pots, as they are difficult to transplant. Set plants 2 feet apart. The plants will need to be replaced after four to five years. It is also grown as an annual. Used as a backdrop for smaller plants and in borders.

Dianthus spp., garden pinks, sweet william

These pinks grow in all regions to 2 feet in height, and bloom May to June in a variety of colors. A light, dry soil in a sunny location is preferred. The seeds, which germinate in one to three weeks, can be planted all during the growing season. Also grown from cuttings or from runner plants. Set plants 1 foot apart. Used for cut flowers, borders, rock gardens, and edging.

Dianthus caryophyllus, carnation

The carnation grows in all regions to 2 feet in height, and blooms in late summer. It prefers a light, well-drained soil in a sunny location. The seeds, which germinate in about one to three weeks, can be sown in late spring. Set plants out 1 foot apart. The plants are cut back in the fall, potted, and held over the winter in a cold frame or some other suitable structure. Sometimes they require supports to climb on. Used for cut flowers, borders, edging, and rock gardens.

Dicentra spp., bleeding heart, Dutchman's breeches

These plants are adapted to the Appalachian mountains and the Piedmont plateau. Growing to 4 feet in height, the flowers range from light pink to red and appear in late spring in clusters scattered over the entire plant. Best suited to shade but will grow in the sun, and prefer a moist soil high in humus. The seeds, which take as long as two months to germinate, can be planted in late autumn. Dicentra may also be grown by dividing the plants or by taking cuttings in the spring. Plants should be set 1 to 1½ feet apart. Used as borders, in front of shrubbery, and as potted plants.

Digitalis purpurea, foxglove

Foxglove grows in all regions to 6 feet in height, with small and numerous tube-shaped white to purple flowers in spikes at the top of the plant from May to July. It does best on a well-drained, rich soil, high in humus, either in the sun or partial shade. Cutting the main flower stem after the flowers dry will encourage new flowers to grow. The seeds, which germinate in three weeks, can be planted from spring to September. Set plants 1 foot apart. This plant is the source of the famed heart-stimulant drug digitalis. Used in borders and for cut flowers.

Gaillardia spp., blanket flower

Gaillardia grows in all regions to 2½ feet in height. The multi-colored flowers are often yellow and maroon, resemble daisies, and bloom from June to November. It does best in full sun on a sandy soil. The seeds, which germinate in about three weeks, can be planted from early spring to late summer. Plants should be set 2 feet apart. If seeds are planted early enough in the spring, plants will bloom the first year; plants divided and replanted will bloom the same year. It may also be grown from root cuttings. Older plants do not produce flowers, so they should be removed. It is also grown as an annual. Used for cut flowers and borders.

Geum chiloense, avens
This plant grows in all regions to 2 feet in height and will bloom from May to October with ball-like clusters of flowers varying from orange-red to yellow. It prefers a sunny location. The seeds, which germinate in about three weeks, can be planted from early spring to midsummer. Plants should be set 1½ feet apart. Used in rock gardens and in borders and for cut flowers.

Gypsophila paniculata, baby's breath
Baby's breath grows in all regions to 4 feet in height and bears white or bluish-white flowers from early summer to early autumn. It comes in single and double flowers. It does best in sunny, dry locations. The seeds, which germinate in one to one and a half weeks, can be planted from early spring to September. Plant at weekly intervals for continuous bloom. Set plants 1 foot apart. It can be grown from cuttings taken in fall or spring. Used in borders and for cut fresh and dried flowers. It is also grown as an annual.

Heuchera sanguinea, coral-bells
This plant grows in all regions to 2 feet in height and is distinguished by attractive evergreen leaves and bright red, bell-shaped flowers, borne on spikes which bloom all summer. It prefers a sunny location with loamy soil. The seeds, which germinate in about one and a half weeks, can be planted in early spring or late fall. The plants can be divided and replanted in the autumn, in a frame, and protected for the winter, or by leaf cuttings. Plants should be set 1½ feet apart. Used in borders, rock gardens, and for cut flowers.

Hosta plantaginea, 'Grandiflora,' hosta, plantain lily
Plantain lily grows in all regions to 2 feet in height, with white

lily-like flowers during August to September. It will grow in sun or shade but does best in partial shade. It is propagated by dividing the roots, although the seed may be planted after ripening in the spring or fall. Grown in shaded areas and on the north side of homes. Plant 1 to 2 feet apart.

Iberis sempervirens, edging candytuft

This bushy perennial grows in all regions to 1½ feet in height and blooms from late spring to September. The seeds, which germinate in three weeks, can be planted in early spring or late fall. Set plants 1 foot apart. The dry flowers should be cut back. It is also grown as an annual. This species is fairly resistant to salt spray and is used as a ground cover.

Kniphofia uvaria, red-hot poker, tritoma, torch flower

This plant grows in all regions to 4 feet in height, with red and some yellow tubular-shaped flowers from August to October. It prefers a sunny location. The seeds, which germinate in three weeks, should be planted in early spring or late fall. Set plants 1½ feet apart. Used in borders and for cut flowers.

Lathyrus latifolius, L. odoratus, sweet pea

L. latifolius grows in all regions to 5 to 6 feet in height, with pink, white, and rose flowers appearing from March to July. Removing the flowers as they mature will prolong blooming. It will grow in almost any soil in sun. The seeds, which germinate in about three weeks, can be planted in early spring. The vines may need staking. The heat-resistant varieties will do better in the Carolinas. It is also grown as an annual. Used for fence and trellis covers and for cut flowers. Planting distance is 2 feet.

Liatris pycnostachya, gayfeather

Gayfeather grows in all regions to 5 feet in height, with rosy-purple flowers in spikes, in the summer or early fall, and will grow in almost any soil and exposure. The seeds germinate in three weeks and can be planted in early spring or late fall. Set plants 1½ feet apart. The roots may also be divided and replanted. Used in borders and for cut flowers.

Limonium latifolium, sea lavender

This plant grows in all regions to 2 feet in height. The blue flowers appear on short spikes at the top of the stem during summer. The leaves grow at the base near the ground, and resemble dandelion leaves. It prefers a sunny location. The seeds germinate in about two weeks and should be planted in early spring. Plants should be set 2½ feet apart. Used for cut flowers, dried flowers, and bedding.

Linum perenne, flax

Flax grows in all regions to 2 feet in height, with numerous white to blue flowers from May to September. It grows in any good garden soil, in the sun. The seeds, which germinate in three to four weeks, can be planted all during the growing season. It may also be grown from division of the plants. Set plants 1½ feet apart. Used for bedding and rock gardens.

Lupinus polyphyllus, lupine

This very erect plant grows in all regions to 3 feet in height. The blue, white, or pink flowers grow in 12-inch-long spikes, from June to September. It prefers a well-drained soil in sun or partial shade. The seeds, which germinate in about three weeks, can be planted in early spring or late fall. Before planting the seed should be soaked. It can also be grown by dividing but it is hard to transplant. Set plants about 2 feet apart. These are also grown as an annual. Used for cut flowers and borders.

Mertensia virginica, Virginia cowslip, Virginia bluebells

This plant grows in all regions, to 2 feet in height, with drooping bell-shaped blue or purple flowers appearing in late June. It prefers a deep, loamy soil in a shaded area and may be grown from seeds, which germinate in a week, or by dividing the plants. The plants should be transplanted when dormant. Used in borders, and planted 1 foot apart.

Monarda didyma and *M. fistulosa,* bee balm horsemint

These plants grow in all regions to 3 feet in height, with summer-blooming red, white, blue, or purple flowers. The leaves have a mint-like aroma. They will grow in almost any soil, but especially moist soils, and are adapted to sun or partial shade. The seeds, which germinate in about two weeks, can be planted in the spring or summer. Plants can be divided and replanted in the spring. Set plants 1 to 1½ feet apart. To encourage blooming cut back the dead flowers, and new blossoms will appear. Used in borders.

Paeonia officinalis, peony

The peony does best in the Appalachian mountains and the Piedmont plateau. It may grow from 2 to 4 feet in height, with several different types of flowers, blooming from late spring to early summer, and requires a well-drained, heavy loam. It is usually better to grow the peony from tubers, which should be divided and set in late fall at least 3 feet apart and 2 to 3 inches deep. Used in borders and for cut flowers.

Papaver nudicaule, Iceland poppy

The Iceland poppy grows in the Appalachian mountains and the Piedmont plateau, reaching a height of 1 foot. The summer-blooming flowers may be yellow, white, or orange. A sandy, deep loam and sun are preferred. The seeds, which germinate in about ten days, can be planted in early spring to summer. Thin to ½ to 1 foot apart as they do not transplant well. It may be propagated by dividing the plants or by root cuttings. It is also grown as an annual. Used in borders for cut flowers.

Papaver orientale, Oriental poppy

This plant grows in the Appalachian mountains and the Piedmont plateau to 4 feet in height. The showy flowers come in a variety of colors, and bloom May to June. A deep loam with open sun is preferred. The seeds, which germinate in ten days, can be planted in early spring. Plants may also be grown from 2-inch cuttings. Also grown as an annual. Used in borders and for cut flowers.

Penstemon spp., penstemon

Penstemon grows in all regions to 2 feet in height, with tubular-shaped, red flowers, which bloom throughout the summer. It prefers shade and well-drained, dry, deep soil. The seeds, which germinate in about ten days, can be planted in early spring or late fall. If planted early, plants may bloom the first season. Set plants 1½ feet apart. It may also be grown from cuttings, or root divisions taken in the fall. Used in borders and for cut flowers.

Phlox paniculata, hardy phlox

This phlox grows in all regions to 3 feet in height and does well in hot, sunny locations. The small, fragrant, multi-colored flowers grow in clusters at the tops of the stems, in early summer. The seeds, which germinate in three to four weeks, should be refrigerated a month before planting in late fall or early winter. Set plants 2 feet apart. The plants should be watered during the dry season, but do not let the foliage get damp, since wetness encourages mildew. It is also grown as an annual. Used for cut flowers and against walls and fences.

Phlox subulata, moss phlox, creeping phlox

This phlox grows in all regions, to 6 inches in height in a clump about 12 inches in diameter. Purple or white flowers appear in May or June. It prefers an acid soil and sun, but will grow in partial shade. Although somewhat drought-resistant, it needs to be watered regularly for best growth. It is propagated by stolons which are planted 8 inches apart, and can also be grown by divisions or from cuttings. As the clump grows in diameter the plants in the center die and should be replanted. Used along walks and as a ground cover.

Platycodon grandiflorum, balloonflower

The balloonflower grows in all regions to 3 feet in height, an erect plant with blue or white flowers that blooms from spring until frost. The flower buds resemble balloons, thus the name. It prefers a sandy loam in sun. The seeds, which germinate in ten days, can be planted any time during the growing season. Set plants 1 foot apart. Do not cut back the dead tops. Dividing the roots is not recommended, because it is difficult. Used as borders and for cut flowers.

Primula spp., primrose

Primula grows in the Appalachian mountains and the Piedmont plateau from 6 to 9 inches in height, and blooms in April or May. A well-drained, rich soil in partial or full shade is preferred. The seeds, which germinate in about three weeks, should be planted in late autumn or early winter. Plants should be set 1 foot apart. Plants may be divided soon after flowering or later in the fall, and replanted. Used as edging, for cut flowers, and in rock gardens.

Pyrethrum roseum, painted daisy, chrysanthemum

This plant grows in all regions to about 2 feet in height with fern-like foliage and various-colored flowers ranging from white to dark red which bloom April to June. It prefers a well-drained area in sun. The seeds, which germinate in three weeks, can be planted any time during the growing season. The plants may also be divided and replanted. Set the plants 1½ feet apart. Used in borders and for cut flowers.

Rudbeckia speciosa, coneflower

Coneflower grows in all regions to 3 feet in height with yellow flowers from August to September. The plants grow on any soil in sun or partial shade and do well in hot areas. The seeds, which germinate in about three weeks, can be planted during the growing season. The plants can be divided and replanted. Set the plants 2½ feet apart. It is also grown as an annual, and is used in borders, bedding, and for cut flowers.

Salvia spp., meadow sage, blue salvia

These plants grow in all regions to 4 feet in height, with blue flowers which bloom from August to frost. The seeds, which germinate in about two weeks, should be planted in the spring. Plants should be set 1½ feet apart.

Sedum spp., stonecrop

Stonecrop grows in all regions to 1½ feet in height, and forms a solid mass of gray-green foliage with yellow, purple, or white flowers. It prefers dry, sandy, loamy soils in a sunny location. It is propagated by rooting pieces of the plants. Tops die back over winter. The recommended species are *S. acre, S. reflexum,* and *S. sarmentosum.*

Stokesia laevis, Stoke's aster

This plant grows in all regions to 1½ feet in height with multi-colored flowers which bloom from July until frost. It prefers a light, well-drained soil in sun. The seeds, which germinate in about three weeks, should be planted very early in the spring in order to bloom the first year. Plants should be set 1½ feet apart. Used as borders and for cut flowers.

Veronica spicata, speedwell

Speedwell grows in the Appalachian mountains and the Piedmont plateau in sun to 1½ feet in height, with blue flowers in spikes from June to July. The seeds, which germinate in about two weeks, can be planted during the growing season. Set plants 1½ feet apart. Used in borders and rock gardens, and for cut flowers.

Vinca spp., periwinkle

These plants grow in all regions to 1½ feet in height, with star-shaped lilac, pink, or white flowers from June to November. They prefer a sunny location but will grow in partial shade, and require adequate moisture. They grow in almost any soil. The seeds, which germinate in two weeks, should be planted after the last frost. Set plants 1 foot apart. They spread also by runners and creeping roots, and are often used as a ground cover.

Viola cornuta, tufted pansy

This plant grows in all regions as a clump to 1 foot in height, and blooms any time from April to October. It grows in sun and partial shade. The seeds, which germinate in about ten days, can be planted during the growing season. Set plants 1 foot apart. Removing the dry flowers will encourage the growth of new blossoms. It is also grown as an annual. Used in edging, bedding, and as a window plant.

RECOMMENDED REFERENCES

Department of Horticulture, *Growing Larkspurs in North Carolina*. North Carolina State University, Raleigh, N.C. 27607, August 1958.

Department of Pathology, *Diseases of Annual Larkspur in North Carolina*. Plant Pathology Information Note 111, North Carolina State University, Raleigh, N.C. 27607.

————, *Diseases of Carnations in North Carolina*. Plant Pathology Information Note 112, North Carolina State University, Raleigh, N.C. 27607.

North Carolina Agricultural Extension Service, *Geranium Culture*. Horticultural Information Leaflet No. 416, North Carolina State University, Raleigh, N.C. 27607, November 1965.

————, *Pansy Culture*. Horticultural Information Leaflet No. 409, North Carolina State University, Raleigh, N.C. 27607, October 1965.

————, *Peonies*. Horticultural Information Leaflet No. 413, North Carolina State University, Raleigh, N.C. 27607.

U. S. Department of Agriculture, *Growing Carnations*. Home and Garden Bulletin No. 86, Washington, D.C. 20250, July 1971.

————, *Growing Flowering Perennials*. Home and Garden Bulletin No. 114, Washington, D.C. 20250, March 1970.

————, *Growing Pansies*. Home and Garden Bulletin No. 149, Washington, D.C. 20250, September 1970.

————, *Growing Peonies*. Home and Garden Bulletin No. 126, Washington, D.C. 20250, May 1971.

CHAPTER 11

Annuals

Annuals are ornamentals that complete their life cycle, from seed to seed, in one growing season. Some are ordinarily biennials, plants that usually produce flowers the second year of growth, but which may flower the first year under certain growing conditions.

The number of species and varieties of annuals available to the gardener is staggering. There are annuals for every part of the garden, whether in sunlight or shade. There are more colors than in the rainbow. Some bear few flowers, others bear a bouquet on each stalk. Flowers of every shape are available, singles and doubles included.

One of the nice things about annuals is their short life span. If some choice proves disappointing one season, it can be easily replaced the following year.

USE

Probably the most attractive feature annuals provide in the garden is a steady array of color, from early spring until first frost.

A mass of brightly colored annuals can be planted below a line of shrubs to brighten the shrub foliage. We have snaps in our daffodil beds so that when the early-blooming daffodils are gone, we have a new parade of color to enjoy.

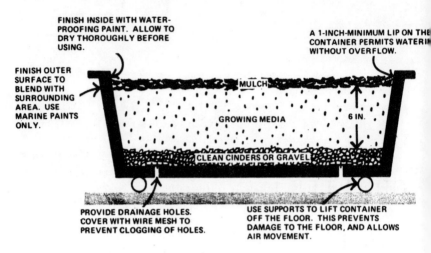

FINISH INSIDE WITH WATER-
PROOFING PAINT. ALLOW TO
DRY THOROUGHLY BEFORE
USING.

A 1-INCH-MINIMUM LIP ON THE
CONTAINER PERMITS WATERIN
WITHOUT OVERFLOW.

FINISH OUTER
SURFACE TO
BLEND WITH
SURROUNDING
AREA. USE
MARINE PAINTS
ONLY.

MULCH

GROWING MEDIA

6 IN.

CLEAN CINDERS OR GRAVEL

PROVIDE DRAINAGE HOLES.
COVER WITH WIRE MESH TO
PREVENT CLOGGING OF HOLES.

USE SUPPORTS TO LIFT CONTAINER
OFF THE FLOOR. THIS PREVENTS
DAMAGE TO THE FLOOR, AND ALLOWS
AIR MOVEMENT.

68. Preparing a planter for use (Courtesy U. S. Department
of Agriculture)

Planted among young shrubs, annuals brighten the area until the
shrubs fill in. Mass plantings are attractive eye-fillers; edging along
areas is another practical use for annuals.

Some gardeners use annuals in wooden, brick, and concrete plant
containers (Figure 68).

SELECTING KINDS OF PLANTS

In selecting kinds and varieties be sure to keep in mind the light
situation and base your selection on that consideration.

A light meter, calibrated in foot candles (FC), can help you determine the quantity of light in a specific locale.

Full sunlight is 3,000 FC or higher during the day with no shading.

Partial sunlight is 1,200 to 3,000 FC with some shading during the
day.

Light shade is 500 to 1,200 FC resulting from light filtering
through the foliage or screen.

Dense shade is 100 to 500 FC with no direct sunlight.

Some grasses and a few plants will survive dense shade; we have
found *Colutea arborescens* to flourish under such conditions but
generally most plants will not survive less than 100 FC.

OBTAINING PLANTS

The two ways to get annual plants for your garden are either to grow your own or buy started plants.

Home-grown

If your start your own plants seed can be sown at the recommended time in a prepared seedbed. There is no shortage of sources of good flower seed in the Carolinas. It is suggested that seed be bought close to planting time to minimize storing time at home. Seed can be stored in containers in the family refrigerator if necessary.

If you have a space, or an indoor garden, you can start seeds indoors; cold frames and hotbeds are often used for an early start.

The new hybrids are slightly more expensive than inbred varieties, but they usually are more vigorous and produce more and larger flowers. The cost of seed is a very small part of the total cost of a garden and the slightly higher seed cost is usually worthwhile.

Buying Plants

Started plants, usually in bloom, are widely available in garden shops and nurseries, as well as in supermarkets and grocery stores.

Be sure the plants look healthy and thrifty and have been cared for. Those sold in plant bands can be planted in their containers in the garden area.

SOIL PREPARATION

Good soil preparation should begin in the fall. Just as for other plants, good drainage is an indispensable requirement. A simple test is to dig a hole 12 inches deep in the proposed bedsite, and fill it with water. If it drains overnight permeability is good.

When the bedsite is ready, deep spading and removal of rocks, twigs, and trash should be completed. Peat moss or any other decayed organic matter should then be added. Spading can be done one or two times more during the dormant season. If weeds appear remove them with all of the root system. Just before planting add fertilizer, and lime if needed, 3 pounds per 100 square feet is suggested.

If the water drainage is poor there are several practical remedies available. One is to raise the level of the plant bed by digging furrows around it and putting the soil from the furrows on top of the bed. In addition good topsoil from another source can be used to raise the bed. Such raised beds do require closer attention to water needs, as they may dry out.

Another but more tedious method would be to dig out an area larger than the bed, lay down a 6-inch layer of sand, and then refill. This would create a raised bed.

Level the top of the bed, rake it smooth, and you are ready to sow seed or set started plants.

Planting

TIME

An average soil temperature of 60° F. is optimum for germination of most annual plant seed. A number, however, can be sown slightly earlier, when the soil is in workable condition. These few include coneflower, stock, strawflower, sweet pea, and sweet alyssum.

In almost all cases, the earliest planting date would fall sometime after the average date for the last frost in your area (see Chapter 2).

It is possible to sow seed several times during the growing season and have a continuous series of flowers.

SEED

If your soil has a tendency to crust over, make one or more narrow furrows the length of the seedbed using the end of a hoe handle, and fill the furrow with vermiculite. Sow the seed in the furrow and cover lightly with more vermiculite. Water gently by spray to keep from washing away the seed or the vermiculite.

When two true leaves appear, as distinguished from the two parts of the seed, or the cotyledons, thin the plants to the proper distance, to provide for adequate light, nutrients, and water. The thinned seedlings, if removed with care, can be planted elsewhere in the garden.

STARTED PLANTS

Most annuals are sold in plant bands, which help reduce transplanting shock. However, if you buy an entire flat of plants without plant bands, each plant should be cut out with its own block of soil, and then set in its planting hole. If you buy plants in clay pots or tin cans, gently remove them, with their soil as intact as possible, by gently turning the pot upside down and tapping the edge of the pot or can on a solid object, holding your hand to catch the plant as it is loosened.

A nutrient "starter" solution applied at planting time can give the young plants a quick start. To make a "starter" solution dissolve 2 tablespoons of 5–10–5 or 6–12–6 in 1 gallon of water, and apply 1 cup per plant.

WATERING

Water as often as your judgment and experience indicate is needed. Too much water is as troublesome as too little.

PLANTS

Ageratum spp., ageratum

Growing from ½ to 1½ feet in height, this bushy plant with blue and white flowers blooms from June to November. It prefers a sunny location but will grow in partial shade. The seeds, planted after the last frost, germinate within a week, and plants are then set out 1 foot apart. To encourage plants to become bushy and bear more flowers, pinch the tops. Remove dead flowers to prolong blooming.

Antirrhinum spp., snapdragon

Growing from 2 to 3 feet in height, snaps can become branchy and produce more heads if the tips are pinched back before blooming. The seeds planted in the spring or late fall germinate in two weeks and plants are set out about 6–10 inches apart. In mild areas they die back over winter and come back in the spring, and bloom again. Growth is good in sun and partial shade.

Calendula spp., calendula

This bushy plant grows in sun or shade to 1½ feet in height, with yellow flowers from June to November. Seeds, planted in early spring or late fall, germinate in about ten days, and plants should be spaced about 1 foot apart.

Centaurea cyanus, cornflower

Growing to 3 feet in height, cornflower blooms from June to September in sun or partial shade. The seeds, planted in early spring, germinate within a week and plants should be set out about 1 foot apart.

Coleus spp., coleus

Coleus is grown for its beautiful dark green leaves with bright green margins and will grow to 2 feet. It prefers a sunny location but will grow in partial shade. The seeds, planted after the last frost, or started indoors earlier, germinate in about a week and should be set outdoors about 1 foot apart.

Coreopsis tinctoria, calliopsis

This bushy plant grows in sun or partial shade to 3 feet in height, with yellow flowers blooming from June to October. The seeds, planted after the last frost, germinate in a week and plants should be set out about 1 foot apart.

Cosmos spp., cosmos

This bushy plant can grow to 6 feet in height in the sun. It blooms from July to November. The seeds, planted as soon as danger of frost is over, germinate within a week, and plants should be spaced 1 foot apart.

Gomphrena globosa, globe amaranth

Globe amaranth grows to 2 feet in height, with purple and white flowers appearing from July to October. It prefers sun. The seeds, planted in early spring when frost danger is over, germinate in about two weeks, and plants should be spaced about 1 foot apart.

Gypsophila paniculata, baby's breath

The varieties grown as annuals reach a height of 1½ feet, with pink or white flowers. (For more information see chapter on perennials.)

Helianthus annuus, sunflower

This familiar erect yellow flower grows from 4 to 7 feet in height, and blooms in July and August. It prefers a sunny location. The seeds planted after last frost germinate in five days, and plants should be spaced 1 foot apart, or farther, for larger varieties.

Impatiens balsamina, garden balsam

Growing to 1 foot in height, this plant is an annual as well as perennial. It prefers partial or full shade. The seeds, planted after frost danger is over, or started indoors, germinate in about two weeks, and plants should be spaced 1 foot apart after the danger of last frost is well past.

Ipomoea purpurea, morning-glory

This vine grows to 4 feet in height and blooms from June to November. It does best in shady areas but will adapt to sunny locations. The seeds, planted when frost danger is past, germinate in about five days, and plants should be set out about 3 feet apart. The plant reseeds itself, not always desirable.

Lobularia maritima, sweet alyssum

This spreading annual grows to a foot in height, and has white flowers appearing from May to November. It prefers a sunny location and well-drained soil. The seeds, planted in early spring, germinate within a week, and plants should be set out about 1 foot apart.

Matthiola incana, stock

A bushy annual which grows to 2½ feet in height, stock blooms from June to August. It prefers a sunny location. The seed, which germinates in about five days, should be planted from February to April for early blooming, and July to September for late blooming, depending on altitude. It can be protected over winter and will grow the second year.

Petunia hybrida, petunia

A bushy annual growing to 2 feet in height which adapts to a range of sites, petunia blooms from May to November. The seeds may be started indoors as early as February and germinate in about ten days. Plants should be spaced about 1 foot apart after the last frost is past. Started plants are readily available at nurseries.

Portulaca pilosa, portulaca, garden purslane

A creeping annual that grows to about 9 inches in height in the sun and blooms from June to October. The seeds planted after the last frost or in the fall germinate within ten days. It is very good for hot areas. Planting distance is 1 foot apart.

Salpiglossis sinuata, painted-tongue

This bushy annual grows in sun or partial shade to 3 feet in height and blooms from June to November. It does not like extreme temperatures. The seeds, planted from March to May, germinate in about two weeks. Planting distance is 1 foot apart.

Salvia splendens, scarlet sage

It grows to 3 feet in height, with red and blue flowers from June to November. It prefers a sunny location. The seeds, planted in March to May, germinate in about two weeks. Planting distance is 1 foot.

Scabiosa atropurpurea, scabious

Growing to 3 feet in height, this bushy annual blooms from June to November. It prefers a sunny location. The seeds, planted in the spring or summer, germinate in about one week. Planting distance is 1 foot.

Tagetes spp., marigold

This familiar bushy annual with yellow flowers blooming from June to November may grow to 4 feet in height and prefers a sunny location. The seeds, planted after the last frost, germinate within a week. Planting distance is 1 foot.

Tropaeolum majus, nasturtium

There are both bush and vine varieties that can grow from 1 to 8 feet in height, with flowers from May to November. Nasturtium prefer a sunny location in a well-drained soil of low fertility. The seeds, planted after last frost, germinate within a week. Plants are set out 1 foot apart.

Verbena spp., verbena

Also grown as a perennial, this creeping plant grows to a foot in height. It blooms from June to October and prefers a sunny location. The seeds, planted after last frost, germinate in about three weeks. Plants should be set out 1½ to 2 feet apart. The tops can be cut back to encourage branching.

Zinnia spp., zinnia

This very bushy annual grows from 2 to 3 feet in height and blooms from June to November. It does best in a sunny location, and tolerates heat. The foliage is susceptible to mildew, so avoid unnecessary wetting. The seeds, planted after last frost, germinate within five days. Planting distance is 1 foot apart.

RECOMMENDED REFERENCES

Department of Pathology, *Diseases of Snapdragons in North Carolina*. Plant Pathology Information Note 113, North Carolina State University, Raleigh, N.C. 27607.

North Carolina Agricultural Extension Service, *Snapdragon Leafspot Caused by Cercospora antirrhina*. Technical Bulletin No. 179, North Carolina State University, Raleigh, N.C. 27607.

U. S. Department of Agriculture, *Growing Flowering Annuals*. Home and Garden Bulletin No. 91, Washington, D.C. 20250, March 1970.

CHAPTER 12

Bulbs and Other Underground Parts

Bulbs are adapted to a wide range of elevations and rainfall and require little care to brighten a corner of a lawn or garden. They can be used as border plants along a driveway, in masses for a burst of color, as foundation plantings and around shrubs, and as potted plants.

Bulbs

We have used the term "bulb" to designate particular underground plant parts used as a means of propagation. Actually there are other underground plant parts used for propagation, which differ in structure and have different "official" names.

Bulbs, such as seen in onion, gladiolus, and lily, are made up of telescoped rings or layers. As the plant begins to grow the "telescope" pushes out from the center.

Corms are underground stems, thick, fleshy, growing upright, seen in gladioli. Each year a new corm is produced by the plant, above the old one.

Tubers are underground, fleshy, modified stems or roots, with buds or eyes, seen in the dahlia and potato. Tubers lacking eyes will not grow.

Rhizomes are underground stems, usually horizontal, with buds, as found in canna and some irises.

Successful Growing

Steps in growing bulbs successfully include buying healthy, disease-and insect-free planting material (Figure 69), proper storage in a cool, fairly dry place, 60° F. to 65° F., proper preparation of the planting site (Figure 70) including a cone of peat moss at the bottom of each planting hole, planting at the depth recommended for the kind of bulb (Figures 71, 72), planting upright (Figure 73), and regular watering and proper fertilizer use.

For bulbs left in the ground over winter, a mulch of pine needles, leaves, or straw can provide protection from alternate freezing and thawing damage.

During the growing season watering at regular intervals will help produce attractive, good-size flowers. A weed-free bed is another essential.

At the end of flowering the drying flower stalks should be cut back so that plant food goes into the bulb rather than into seed production.

Time of Flowering

Bulbs can be divided into two groups, fall-planted spring-flowering (Table 4), and spring-planted summer-flowering (Table 5) varieties.

In most areas of the Carolinas spring-flowering bulbs can be planted in the fall to give the roots a chance to become established before the ground freezes, but late enough to see that the bulbs do not begin aboveground growth.

Summer-flowering bulbs are planted in the spring after the damage of frost is over, from March to May. Some are started indoors in winter or early spring in flats or pots, including begonia, caladium, calla, canna, gloxinia, and some lycoris.

Bulbs and related structures planted in a southern exposure near a wall or a building will bloom earlier than those in a northern exposure, because of higher temperatures.

Soils

An easy test to determine if a proposed site has adequate drainage is to dig a hole a foot deep and fill it with water. If the water drains away overnight, drainage is adequate; if water remains in the hole the bed should be raised by adding several inches of soil.

Soil operations such as digging and planting are best done when the soil is dry and crumbly. Use a garden spade to dig down to

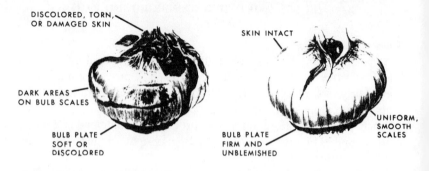

DISCOLORED, TORN, OR DAMAGED SKIN

SKIN INTACT

DARK AREAS ON BULB SCALES

BULB PLATE SOFT OR DISCOLORED

BULB PLATE FIRM AND UNBLEMISHED

UNIFORM, SMOOTH SCALES

69. Signs of an unhealthy and healthy bulb (Photo courtesy U. S. Department of Agriculture)

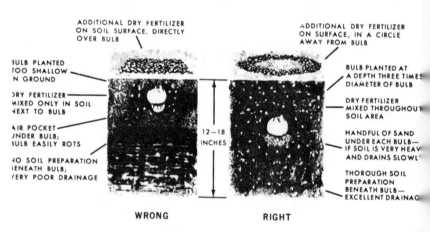

ADDITIONAL DRY FERTILIZER ON SOIL SURFACE, DIRECTLY OVER BULB

ADDITIONAL DRY FERTILIZER ON SURFACE, IN A CIRCLE AWAY FROM BULB

BULB PLANTED TOO SHALLOW IN GROUND

BULB PLANTED AT A DEPTH THREE TIMES DIAMETER OF BULB

DRY FERTILIZER MIXED ONLY IN SOIL NEXT TO BULB

DRY FERTILIZER MIXED THROUGHOUT SOIL AREA

AIR POCKET UNDER BULB; BULB EASILY ROTS

HANDFUL OF SAND UNDER EACH BULB— IF SOIL IS VERY HEAVY AND DRAINS SLOWLY

NO SOIL PREPARATION BENEATH BULB; VERY POOR DRAINAGE

THOROUGH SOIL PREPARATION BENEATH BULB— EXCELLENT DRAINAGE

12–18 INCHES

WRONG

RIGHT

70. Planting procedure and preparation of planting site (Photo courtesy U. S. Department of Agriculture)

10 or 12 inches. Rocks should be removed but leaves and organic material turned under to decay and enrich the soil.

For an area of 100 square feet, use two cups of 5–10–10 fertilizer, about a 1-inch layer of sand, and a 1-inch layer of peat moss. Incorporate these materials into the bulb bed with a spade or shovel.

Be sure to plant the bulbs with the growing point up, and with the soil packed firmly around and below the bulb. Water thoroughly after planting, and fill up any holes that appear.

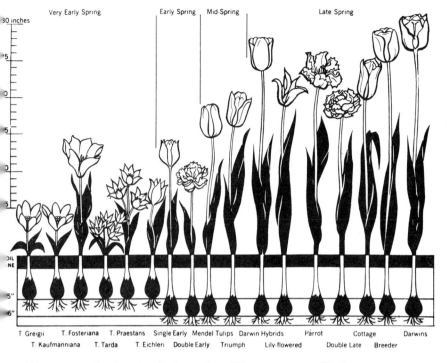

71. Proper planting depth for tulips (Photo courtesy U. S. Department of Agriculture)

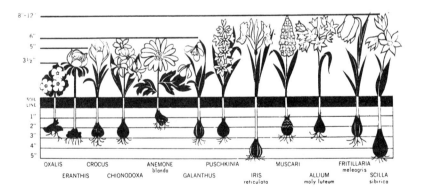

72. Proper planting depth for various bulbs (Photo courtesy U. S. Department of Agriculture)

73. Proper spacing and placing the bulb upright is important
(Photo courtesy U. S. Department of Agriculture)

Forcing Bulbs

In years gone by New York City public schools would have an annual fall narcissus bulb sale. Children would take a bulb home, pot it in gravel, store the pot in a closet, and water carefully.

When the first green shoots appeared, joy reigned and the bulbs were then put in a kitchen on a windowsill to get sunlight, even in the brick canyons of New York. Each green shoot was watched closely and breathlessly and when the aromatic flowers finally ap-

74. Growing or forcing bulbs in the home is fun. Here are hyacinth bulbs in a special hyacinth glass. The water should just touch the bottom of the bulb, as shown in the left-hand glass. Container should be kept in a cool, dark place, above freezing, at around 40° F. When the flower buds begin to develop and grow, move the bulbs to a cool, bright spot, 55° to 65° F. Blooming will occur in about one month. (Photo courtesy U. S. Department of Agriculture)

peared great was the rejoicing. Money was scarce in the days of the Great Depression, but almost all families squeezed out a few cents for each child to be able to have his own bulb. The first author was one of those kids and remembers well the planning and corner cutting to scrape together the needed pennies.

That procedure is known as forcing—providing conditions for indoor growth earlier than nature permits outdoors. The best bulbs for forcing are the old favorites, narcissus, crocus, hyacinth, and tulip (Figure 74). Others can be tried as well.

75. Forcing bulbs can begin out of doors. In November plant bulbs in pots in a good potting mixture. The pots should be buried out of doors in a cool spot, under a shrub or tree. Set the pots close together and cover them with soil to a depth of 3 or 4 inches. Then place hardwood screen over the pots to protect them from rats, mice, and moles. After eight weeks in the mountains to twelve weeks on the coast, when shoots appear, bring the bulbs indoors. (Photo courtesy U. S. Department of Agriculture)

We have already given the two phases of forcing—the dark, cool phase at a temperature of 40° F., usually in a closet, or outdoors (Figure 75). This phase, beginning in October or November, is continued for eight to twelve weeks. The soil should be kept moist.

When the shoots appear, in December or January, the second phase begins. During this time the bulbs are moved to a warmer area in light. Blooming will take place in four to six weeks.

Instead of planting the bulbs of narcissus, crocus, hyacinth, and tulip in the dark and cold outdoors, they can be kept in a refrigerator for eight weeks. At the end of that time the second phase begins.

76. Digging, cleaning, and storing bulbs for winter (U. S.
Department of Agriculture photograph by Purdy)

Once a bulb has been forced it should be thrown away.

Care of Propagating Material

In the higher elevations of the Carolinas and in the Piedmont
bulbs can remain in the ground much longer than in the coastal areas
of South Carolina. If growth is vigorous and the bulbs become
jammed together in time they should be dug in the late fall and
stored until time to plant (Figure 76).

In digging bulbs for replanting be sure they are mature. Wait until the tops turn yellow-brown, then carefully examine some of the bulbs without removing them. If their coats are brown they are ready to collect. It is a good idea to reduce water application frequency prior to lifting.

The bulbs can be spread to dry on newspaper in a shady, ventilated area, such as a carport. When they are dried store them in a cool area but not below 50° F.

Depth of Planting

The proper depth of planting is important to normal development. Tables 4 and 5 give this information, as do Figures 71 and 72. A special chart for tulips is given showing plant heights and depth of bulb placement recommended.

77. Proper method of cutting flowers (Courtesy U. S. Department of Agriculture)

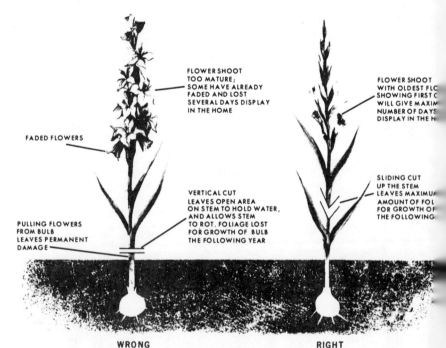

FLOWER SHOOT
TOO MATURE;
SOME HAVE ALREADY
FADED AND LOST
SEVERAL DAYS DISPLAY
IN THE HOME

FLOWER SHOOT
WITH OLDEST FLO
SHOWING FIRST C
WILL GIVE MAXIM
NUMBER OF DAYS
DISPLAY IN THE H

FADED FLOWERS

SLIDING CUT
UP THE STEM
LEAVES MAXIMUM
AMOUNT OF FOL
FOR GROWTH OF
THE FOLLOWING

VERTICAL CUT
LEAVES OPEN AREA
ON STEM TO HOLD WATER,
AND ALLOWS STEM
TO ROT. FOLIAGE LOST
FOR GROWTH OF BULB
THE FOLLOWING YEAR

PULLING FLOWERS
FROM BULB
LEAVES PERMANENT
DAMAGE

WRONG   RIGHT

Flower Harvest

Improper collecting of flowers can permanently damage bulbs and set them back. The proper method of cutting flowers is no more troublesome than an improper method (Figure 77).

RECOMMENDED REFERENCES

Department of Pathology, *Diseases of Gladioli in North Carolina.* Plant Pathology Information Note 166, North Carolina State University, Raleigh, N.C. 27607.

―――, *Diseases of Iris in North Carolina.* Plant Pathology Information Note 110, North Carolina State University, Raleigh, N.C. 27607.

North Carolina Agricultural Extension Service, *Bearded Iris Culture.* Horticultural Information Leaflet No. 420, North Carolina State University, Raleigh, N.C. 27607, July 1970.

―――, *Dahlias.* Horticultural Information Leaflet No. 408, North Carolina State University, Raleigh, N.C. 27607, August 1971.

―――, *Fall Planted Spring Flowering Bulbs.* Horticultural Information Leaflet No. 524, North Carolina State University, Raleigh, N.C. 27607, August 1971.

―――, *Growing Caladiums.* Horticultural Information Leaflet No. 525, North Carolina State University, Raleigh, N.C. 27607, November 1971.

―――, *Growing Tulips.* Horticultural Information Leaflet No. 289, North Carolina State University, Raleigh, N.C. 27607, October 1965.

U. S. Department of Agriculture, *Growing Dahlias.* Home and Garden Bulletin No. 131, Washington, D.C. 20250, October 1970.

―――, *Growing Iris in the Home Garden.* Home and Garden Bulletin No. 66, Washington, D.C. 20250, April 1971.

―――, *Spring Flowering Bulbs.* Home and Garden Bulletin No. 136, Washington, D.C. 20250, January 1971.

―――, *Summer Flowering Bulbs.* Home and Garden Bulletin No. 151, Washington, D.C. 20250, February 1971.

TABLE 4   INFORMATION FOR PLANTING OF SPRING-FLOWERING BULBS

KIND	PLANTING Depth	Spacing	COMMENTS
Crocus (*Crocus* spp.)	3"-5"	3"-4"	Early spring bloomer. Plant in groups, borders, and garden sites. Leave in place five to ten years. Largest corms produce largest flowers.
Daffodil (*Narcissus bulbocodium*)	4"-8"	6"-10"	Plant in beds, or borders, in front of shrubs.
Glory-of-the-snow (*Chionodoxa* spp.)	3"-5"	3"	Early spring bloomer. In shade of deciduous trees, in lawns, with crocus. Leave in place five years or more.
Hyacinth (*Hyacinthus* spp.)	3"-6"	3"-4"	Late spring bloomer; plant between muscari and tulips.
Iris, Bulbous (*Iris* spp.)	1"-4"	6"-12"	Sun. Used in borders and with shrubs. Rhizomes may be separated after four to five years.
Lily (stem-rooting) Lily (base-rooting) (*Lilium* spp.)	10"	6"-18"	Sun. Results with these are variable. Many kinds of hybrids are available blooming from June to September, and ranging from 2 to 6 feet in height.
Muscari (*Muscari* spp.)	3"-4"	3"-4"	Late spring bloomer; used as ground cover, in rock gardens, and with shrubs.

KIND	PLANTING Depth	PLANTING Spacing	COMMENTS
Narcissus (*Narcissus* spp.)	4"-6"	4"-8"	Mid-spring bloomers; many varieties available; flower beds and borders.
Scilla (*Scilla* spp.)	4"		Planted in clumps, bloom from mid-spring to late spring; used as borders and in beds, in sun to light shade.
Snowdrop (*Galanthus* spp.)	3"-4"	3"-4"	Late winter bloomer; plant in shade with muscari and chionodoxa.
Tulip (*Tulipa* spp.)	4"-6"	6"-8"	Many varieties are available; used in borders and masses.

TABLE 5 INFORMATION FOR PLANTING OF SUMMER-FLOWERING BULBS

KIND	PLANTING Depth	Spacing	COMMENTS
Achimenes (*Achimenes* spp.)			Light shade. Grown in pots and greenhouses.
Amaryllis (*Amaryllis* spp.)	one-half bulb planted	10"-18"	Used as a potted plant and in borders. Plant in clumps of three to five. Dig bulbs in the fall and store in damp peat.
Begonia, tuberous (*Begonia tuberhybrida*)			Light shade, as pot plant and gardens. Start indoors in late winter. Keep in a dark room. After six weeks put in pots or move outdoors. Store tubers over winter in a cool, dark place.
Caladium (*Caladium* spp.)	Cover with 1" peat moss.	close together	Light shade. Keep flower buds removed. Used as pot plants. Plant tuber in a flat or pot in January and keep at 70°F. In the spring move outdoors or in containers.
Calla (*Zantedeschia aethiopica*)	Barely cover in 6" pot. Rhizomes 2"	12"	Used as a pot plant. Start in pots in the early fall. Keep at 50-60°F., watering daily. Reduce watering in the spring. Light shade.
Canna (*Canna* spp.)	Cover with 1" peat moss indoors. In the garden just below the surface.	12"-18"	Full sun. Plant rhizomes during spring in flats of peat moss. Keep them damp. Plant in the garden when danger of frost is gone. Tall varieties need stakes. In the fall dig and dry rhizomes and store over winter.

Kind	Planting Depth	Spacing	Comments
Dahlia (*Dahlia* spp.)	roots 6"-8" seeds ¾"		Borders and beds with six hours or more sunlight. Seeds are planted one month prior to last frost indoors, and transplanted when frost danger is past. Roots are dug in the fall and stored.
Day lily (*Hemerocallis* spp.)	just below soil surface with crown ½" below surface	18"-24" or clumps 3"-4" apart	May be planted from spring to fall. Sun to light shade, will grow on poor soils. The clumps can remain in the garden for four to five years. Plant in masses.
Gladiolus (*Gladiolus* spp.)	4"-7"	6"-8"	Planted in rows or beds. Leave bulbs in the ground for several years. Save bulbs larger than 1" in diameter, and store at about 40°F.
Gloxinia (*Sinningia speciosa*)	5"-6" pots		Pot plants for light shade. Plant bulbs in early spring and keep at 65°F. Place outside after last killing frost.
Iris (*Iris* spp.)	rhizome tops 2" below soil surface in triangle	18"	Sun. Mulch the first season with straw, pine bark, or pine needles. Divide clumps every two to five years, in mid-summer.
Lily (*Lilium* spp.)	3 x bulb height	6"-18"	Sun. Many forms are available, from 2½ to 6 feet tall.

Kind	Planting Depth	Spacing	Comments
Lycoris (*Lycoris* spp.)	4" in garden 6" pots or 6" apart	8"	Light shade, as a garden or flower bed plant, or in pots. Two types with foliage dying in the summer, or living all winter. Dig bulbs in the spring when leaves yellow and store over summer, 35°F. to 45°F.
Peony (*Paeonia* spp.)			Divide roots every six to seven years.
Tuberose (*Polianthes tuberosa*)	2"-3" garden	8"-12"	Sun. Store indoors over winter.

CHAPTER 13

Ground Covers

Ground covers are low-growing plants serving, in a way, to carpet an area when some specific problem exists.

The problem may be a steep slope, a very shaded area, an area subject to heavy use, an area subject to erosion, or an area you want to close to use.

Ground covers can reduce labor and costs as they generally require less maintenance than a grass lawn. The establishment of a ground cover may require slightly more labor in initial planting, but overall they are less expensive. In most cases lawns cannot and should not be replaced by ground cover.

Site Preparation

If the land is too steep for over-all preparation, individual planting holes can be dug, and peat moss or other organic material put into the bottom. The planting holes should be dug deep enough to spread the roots out flat, but close enough to minimize washing and erosion.

On level areas the ground should be worked up thoroughly to a depth of at least 6 inches and more if possible, and every weed rootstock removed. The clearer the area is at the beginning the easier will be subsequent maintenance. The extra labor at the beginning will pay off in reduced labor for several seasons.

When you are satisfied you have done all you can to eliminate weeds, add peat moss, rotted manure, or compost to the soil and work it in well. Use fertilizer suited to your soil type.

Planting on Sloping Hills

If you have relatively low banks consider the use of retaining walls at the bottom of the slope to protect against erosion and keep the slope in place. A properly built wall can be installed by the handy homeowner keeping in mind the details shown in Figure 78. Field tile or any convenient drainage system will allow water to move from the high spots to the low without problems of soil washing.

Selecting Plants

Many plants useful as ground covers can be propagated by the gardener if time and space are available.

Plants should be selected for the specific purpose the gardener has in mind, and should be adapted to the climate as well as the soil type and exposure.

Planting

Setting plants out in the spring is recommended to allow them to get established before winter. Planting, however, can be done any time during the growing season.

The plants should be spaced close enough so they will grow together quickly and carpet the area. This distance will depend on rapidity of growth and how spreading the plant is at maturity. The more plants used, however, the higher the cost, if plants are being bought at a nursery or garden store. A compromise between needs and costs will be a problem for each gardener. Table 6 will be a helpful guide.

Care of Plantings

Established ground-cover plantings require watering, application of fertilizer, mulching, and weed control. Fertilizer should be applied during winter and in spring when growth has begun. To reduce chances of burning damage from fertilizer application, pelleted forms are recommended at a rate suitable for the soil type. It is best to apply the fertilizer when the foliage is dry, to avoid burning.

Even if great care has been taken to eliminate weeds and weed

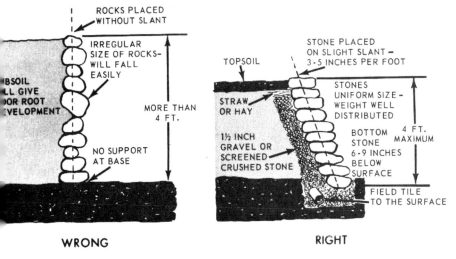

WRONG   RIGHT

78. Retaining wall recommended for sloping hills (Courtesy U. S. Department of Agriculture)

roots prior to planting, weed seeds manage to return. A mulch of suitable material can help control weeds. Be sure that the ground-cover plants are not covered by the mulch.

There is no need to cultivate around ground-cover plants. To do so can slow down the rate of plant growth and their coverage of the soil area.

Regular water applications are essential, particularly during the establishment period. Good judgment and experience will help the gardener to recognize how much water is needed. During the winter, water can be applied on warm days during prolonged dry periods.

Ground covers in the Piedmont and coastal plains region should be protected during the winter with burlap, small pine branches, and such to reduce possibilities of sun injury. If plant tissues freeze and then thaw, they can be damaged. To reduce winter damage, the U. S. Department of Agriculture recommends the use of anti-transpirant spray in the fall to reduce plant water loss during the winter.

Proper care includes pruning dead branches and shoots and removal of dead plants in the spring. Whether to replace dead plants for others to grow in over empty areas will depend on the extent of the area that is affected.

TABLE 6 *The number of plants needed to cover specific areas at different planting distances*

Planting distances, inches	Plants needed per 10 sq. feet
4	90
6	40
8	23

Planting distances, inches	Plants needed per 100 sq. feet
12	100
18	45
24	25
36	10
48	7

PLANTS

Ajuga reptans, bugleweed, carpet bugle

Bugleweed grows in all regions to 6 inches in height and makes rapid growth with little care. It will grow in any exposure but requires extra watering in sunny areas. Flowers may be blue or purple, with leaves turning bronze in the fall. Use twenty plants per square yard. It spreads by runners, and can be propagated by seeds as well. It will grow in 3 to 4 inches of soil spread over paved areas. It can be used as an edging plant and in small beds.

Arctostaphylos uva-ursi, bearberry

This plant is adapted to poor, sandy soils and may be used in rocky or seashore areas. It has small white flowers and evergreen leaves only ½ inch long, and grows to 8 inches in height. It is difficult to transplant and should be transplanted as a sod, or in peat pots. It does well in sun.

Armeria alpina, thrift

Thrift is a perennial that prefers a dry, sandy soil with full sun and is adapted to all regions. The seeds may be planted during the growing season, and spaced 1 foot apart, will germinate in about ten days. Use partial shade until the young plants are sturdy.

Celastrus scandens, bittersweet

Bittersweet grows in the Appalachian mountains as a vigorous vine to 20 feet in length, in good soil. The small, inconspicuous flowers are followed by bright orange-yellow fruits with crimson seeds which persist over winter. It will grow in shade or sun and does well on rocky slopes and banks. Seeds germinate without problem. The fruits are useful for dry arrangements.

Convallaria majalis, lily-of-the-valley

Adapted to all regions, lily-of-the-valley grows to 8 inches in height and prefers rich soil in full sun to partial shade. The plants should be spaced 4 to 6 inches apart. Every four or five years after the tops die down in the fall, dig the plants, separate, and replant. Used as cut flowers, borders, and massed plantings.

Cotoneaster spp., rock spray, cotoneaster

The dwarf forms are recommended as ground covers for use in dry, exposed areas. Use three plants per square yard. (See chapter on perennials.)

Dichondra repens, dichondra, ponyfeet

Dichondra grows in all regions in sun or partial shade, and tolerates summer heat as long as it has moisture. It is recommended for light traffic areas. Heavy frost kills aboveground parts, but it will usually come back from underground stems. It is usually propagated by replanting small clumps, although seed can be used.

Euonymus fortunei, E. radicans, wintercreeper

These evergreen vines root at the stem nodes, and will climb trees and walls. *E. fortunei* grows into a semi-shrub 4 feet in height. It is best in a rather fertile moist soil. Both these species are used as ground covers for banks, and are almost maintenance-free. They can be propagated by layering or planting rooted runners, taken either in spring or in July. Cuttings will root in about four weeks. *E. fortunei* is recommended for use at the seashore, and is planted one plant per square yard; the same distance is used for *E. radicans.*

Galax aphylla, galax

In North Carolina galax grows in the mountains and the Piedmont and in South Carolina it grows in the Piedmont plateau. It grows to about 6 inches in height. This hardy low-growing evergreen grows best in cool, shady areas, though it will grow in partial shade. Plant fifteen to twenty plants per square yard. Older plants can be divided and replanted; some nurseries carry it on hand. It can be planted in the fall or spring. It has long been used in florist arrangements.

Gelsemium sempervirens, Carolina jessamine

This plant grows in the Piedmont and the coastal plain in partial shade, but will adapt to dry, sunny, sandy areas if the soil is enriched with organic matter or topsoil. It is a vigorous grower and should be in out-of-the-way, roomy areas. Plants grow to 2 feet or more in height and should be spaced 2 feet apart. Cuttings of mature wood can be taken in late summer for propagation. It requires yearly pruning.

Genista pilosa, silky-leaf woadwaxen

This plant grows in all regions and adapts well to a poor, sandy, well-drained soil with partial shade. The pea-type yellow flowers appear in May or June.

Hedera helix, English ivy

This familiar evergreen grows in all regions under a wide range of soils and light conditions. To propagate, separate plants and roots and plant in a new site, three rooted cuttings per square yard. Do not use around shrubs because it is a vigorous climber. The solid green leaved varieties are more vigorous and take low temperatures better than the variegated varieties.

Hemerocallis spp., day lily

The day lily grows in all regions in full or partial shade in a variety of soils. The plants should be divided every three to four years. It may be grown from division of the roots or from seed. The seeds, which germinate in two weeks, should be planted about 2 to 2½ feet apart in the fall or early spring.

Hydrangea petiolaris, climbing hydrangea

This beautiful vine grows in all regions to 50 feet in length and has broad, handsome foliage that overlaps in shingle-like fashion, with the white fragrant flowers occurring in large, flat panicles. It will grow in sun to partial shade and is considered drought-resistant. Propagated by cuttings, layering, and seeds planted in flats. Plants should be spaced one per square yard.

Hypericum calycinum, St.-John's-wort

A semi-evergreen growing in all regions, with yellow flowers appearing in midsummer. It grows to 1 foot in height in sun or partial shade, and does well on sandy soil. Plants should be spaced 2 feet apart. Spreading by underground stolons, it can also be grown from cuttings, seeds, or by divisions. The foliage turns red in the fall.

Iris spp., bearded iris

Iris grows in all regions and does well on any well-drained soil. Set the rhizomes about a foot apart in a staggered fashion with all the fans pointing the same direction, so they will spread evenly. Barely cover rhizomes with soil.

Juniperus spp., juniper (Figure 79)

Creeping juniper (*J. horizontalis*) and Japanese garden juniper (*J. procumbens*) are considered best because they are low-growing.

Shore juniper (*J. conferta*) does well on beach plantings as it is salt-spray-tolerant.

All are low shrubs that may be used as a ground cover, and do well on slopes in sunny, dry areas. Spacing is about 18–20 inches apart with mulch between plants. Cuttings are taken in November through February and treated with indole-3-butyric acid solution to help rooting. Foliage color varies from light green to blue.

Liriope muscari, L. spicata, creeping liriope, monkeygrass, lilyturf

This attractive, low-growing, grass-like plant with rather broad dark green foliage and clusters of lavender flowers is good for shaded areas, especially under trees. It can also be grown in full sun. To propagate, separate clumps and groups of individual plants and set 3 to 4 inches apart. Every three or four years the plants should be dug up and separated, and replanted. A number of newer varieties are available, with variegated leaves and differing tolerances to low temperatures.

79. *Juniperus* spp., juniper (Photo courtesy Stern's Nurseries, Geneva, New York)

Lonicera japonica, climbing honeysuckle

Growing in all regions, this hardy shrubby vine has beautiful flowers and an attractive fragrance as well as handsome berries in autumn. The evergreen trumpet honeysuckle, *L. sempervirens,* is especially good as a ground cover. All thrive in a range of soils in sun or shade, and require little attention. Use one plant per square yard. The species *L. henryi* is not as vigorous in growth, and will be useful in restricted areas where the standard honeysuckle would take over a yard or other plants. Annual pruning is required to control spread of all species.

Mitchella repens, partridgeberry, squawberry

This plant grows in all regions and has small, glistening, round, white-streaked leaves with red berries that persist over winter. It is good for moist, shady locations, especially shady rock gardens, and grows to 6 inches in height. It requires a moderately moist soil rich in humus. Divide and plant 6 to 8 inches apart.

Ophiopogon japonicum, mondograss, dwarf lilyturf

This plant grows in all regions in a range of soils and in sun or shade. It spreads by underground rootstalks and grows to a height of 10 inches. If the tops are damaged by the cold, they can be trimmed back. Separate and set the clumps 3 inches apart.

Pachysandra procumbens, pachysandra, Allegheny pachysandra

This plant reaches a height of 8 inches, adapts to light or shade, and prefers moderately fertile soil. It is spread by underground runners, and individual plants should be set out at the rate of six to ten plants per square yard. After eight to ten years dig the plants up, separate, and replant.

Polygonum spp., silver-lace vine, fleecevine, knot weed, fleeceflower

Polygonum grows in all regions. This slender, delicate-looking vine will grow 25–30 feet in a very short time. The flowers appear about midsummer, and grow in stringy clusters that resemble strands of silvery beads. It does best in the sun in a range of soils.

Pueraria thunbergiana, kudzu vine

This legume grows in all regions. It is grown for its soil-holding capacity, particularly on slopes and cut banks. The tops die back over winter. It makes very vigorous growth and should not be planted near shrubs or trees, as it will climb and take over. It must be watched to keep it from taking over. In the Carolinas a familiar sight is a telephone pole draped with kudzu. The roots are a source of starch.

Rosa wichuraiana, R. rugosa, R. hybrida, wichura rose, memorial rose

Grown in all regions, a partly evergreen vine-like shrub with white single-petaled flowers which are 1½ to 2 inches wide. The stems when covered with soil take root easily. It does well on infertile, dry rocky or sandy sites.

The creeping rugosa rose has promise for beach plantings as it has good resistance to salt-spray damage. The foliage turns orange in the fall.

The trailing rose hybrid 'Max Graf' is adapted to sun and has the same characteristics as *R. wichuraiana.*

Roses may be propagated by seed planted in the fall, hardwood or semi-hardwood cuttings taken in the late summer or fall. A light loamy or sandy soil is best for the cuttings, which will sprout and produce leaves before cold weather. Use one plant per square yard.

Santolina spp., lavender cotton

This plant grows in the Appalachian mountains and the Piedmont in well-drained, sunny areas in poor, sandy soil. The pungent silvery-gray foliage sometimes is killed by cold, but will come back. Plant four to five plants per square yard using rooted cuttings or nursery plants. For compact growth cut back severely every other year. Stems may root when they touch the soil. It can be propagated by cuttings before frost in the fall or in the spring. Since it prefers a dry soil, avoid overwatering.

Sedum spp., stonecrop, orpine

A perennial also grown as a ground cover. (See chapter on perennials.)

Symphoricarpos orbiculatus, coralberry, Indian currant

Coralberry grows in all regions, and prefers poor soils, sun or shade. The flowers are small, yellowish-white, the berries purplish-red. It spreads well by underground stems, and may need pruning to keep it low. Plants can be divided and replanted 2 to 3 feet apart.

Trachelospermum jasminoides, star jasmine, Confederate jasmine

A dark evergreen vine with glossy leaves and waxy white, star-shaped, fragrant flowers growing in the Piedmont plateau and the coastal plains. It does best in partial shade but will tolerate full sun.

Vinca spp., periwinkle

A perennial also grown as a ground cover. (See chapter on perennials.)

Viola spp., violets

Species grow in all regions. They do well in poor soils, and are somewhat drought-resistant. Use eighteen to twenty plants per square yard. They grow in all sorts of light conditions and to different heights. Flower color varies.

Viola pedata, bird's-foot violet, likes sun and sandy soil.

Viola odorata, a fragrant species, long-flowering.

RECOMMENDED REFERENCES

North Carolina Agricultural Extension Service, *Ground Covers for North Carolina.* Circular 529, North Carolina State University, Raleigh, N.C. 27607, 1971.

U. S. Department of Agriculture, *Growing Ground Covers.* Home and Garden Bulletin No. 175, Washington, D.C. 20250, January 1970.

CHAPTER 14

Seashore Gardening

A very special and challenging area of the coastal plains region is the actual seashore. With more and more Americans in the Carolinas buying beach homes for vacation spots, retirement homes, and full-time residences, there is a real need to understand the problems and possible solutions involved in gardening under such adverse conditions.

Salt Spray

The most serious obstacle to seashore gardening is the ocean spray, laden with salt, a plant killer and the greatest limiting factor to be faced.

There are several ways in which this problem can be tackled. Probably the best to begin with is the establishment of rows of salt-resistant shrubs perpendicular to the usual direction of the spray movement. (A line of shrubs parallel to the beach will usually serve the purpose of reducing the salt spray.) In this chapter we have identified and described some of those plants recommended for that purpose by the United States Department of Agriculture Soil Conservation Service. Ranking high in salt tolerance are Adam's-needle, elder (Figure 80), hairawn muhly, and sea oats (Figure 81). Once these plants are established, gardening behind their protective barrier is more practical.

80. *Iva imbricata*, elder (Photo courtesy Soil Conservation Service)

81. *Uniola paniculata*, sea oats (Photo courtesy Soil Conservation Service)

If seashore property is bought that has a native protective plant barrier in place be cautious about removing any more plants than is absolutely necessary, both for the sake of conservation, and to keep in place a proven, established barricade of living plant protection.

In planting a salt-spray barrier include a goodly number of evergreens, as their leaves provide twelve months of protection to reduce salt-spray movement.

Sand

Beach sand has little to recommend it as a medium for the growing of garden plants. It meets the minimum requirement of providing anchorage to hold the plants in place, but is deficient in organic matter, soil minerals, and water-holding capacity.

Bringing a beach sand into productivity is a matter of several years of effort and good management.

The most direct method of improving the sand is to bring in good topsoil, and if possible, peat moss or other organic matter. All of this should be incorporated into the top 6–8 inches of beach sand. The amount to be added will depend on the amount available and the cost of transporting the soil from its source to your property. Depending on the area, it can be hand-spaded in, roto-tilled in, or disked in with a light tractor. As this improvement is carried on it is suggested that about 10 pounds of 5–10–10 fertilizer and 25 pounds of limestone be added to each 1,000 square feet of area to be planted.

The planting holes should be dug as described in Figure 82, and then good, rich, organic topsoil or peat moss used to fill them up as the plants are set in. More frequent watering will be required than is usual, and a mulch on the surface of the soil around the base of the plant will help conserve moisture.

Wind

The wind not only carries salt spray but can cause severe sandblast damage. The shrubs planted as a salt-spray protection will to some extent break up the force of the wind, as they become large. Wind-tolerant plants recommended include live oak (Figure 83), yaupon (Figure 84), yucca, devilwood, wax myrtle, pittosporum (Figure 85), euonymus (Figure 86), elaeagnus (Figure 87), and ligustrum.

82. Preparation of a planting hole (Photo courtesy Soil Conservation Service)

83. *Quercus virginiana*, live oak (Photo courtesy Soil Conservation Service)

84. *Ilex vomitoria,* yaupon holly (Photo courtesy Soil Conservation Service)

85. *Pittosporum tobira,* pittosporum (Photo courtesy Soil Conservation Service)

86. *Euonymus japonicus,* euonymus (Photo courtesy Soil Conservation Service)

The most practical way to break up the wind is with a fence. A snow fence is ideally suited. A solid fence would present too large an obstacle and would soon topple over. Openings in the fence break up the force of the wind enough to provide excellent protection. Some homeowners have built windbreaks of concrete blocks or bricks, with space between. This is excellent, but very expensive.

87. *Elaeagnus* spp., elaeagnus (Photo courtesy Soil Conservation Service)

Temperature

The surface temperature of beach sand, as most of us know, is burning hot and is just as much a threat to plants as it is to the soles of our feet. As a garden begins to take shape, the plants will help cool the surface by the shade they cast, and by the increased water-holding capacity of the soil.

The mixing of good topsoil and organic matter into the beach sand will help pull the temperature down, as will watering. Mulches will also help keep the soil surface cooler than otherwise.

Stabilizing Moving Sands

Sand dunes and beach areas have a strange ability to move, unless they are held in place with plants, or barred from moving by physical barriers such as fences. The best protection against dune "marching" is the preservation of as much as possible of the plant life present on any property that is bought on a beach.

The basic step in establishing a stable area in the moving sands would be the planting of adapted grasses. Once they become established, the ecology of the area is measurably improved by the addition of organic matter, the increase of water-holding capacity of the sand, and the provision of some protection for subsequent plantings from wind and salt-spray damage.

Marshbay cordgrass is recommended for the moister lower sand flats; coastal Bermuda grass for replanting of disturbed areas. American beachgrass is recommended for holding in place larger marching dunes until other larger native plants can be added. These would include sea myrtle (Figure 88), bayberry (Figure 89), and redbay (Figure 90), among others. Rattlebox is useful for dune stabilization, but does best between dunes in lower spots, and is somewhat sensitive to salt spray.

88. *Baccharis halimifolia,* sea myrtle (Photo courtesy Soil Conservation Service)

89. *Myrica pensylvanica,* bayberry (Photo courtesy Soil Conservation Service)

Three recommended more permanent grasses used after American beachgrass (Figure 91) are sea oats, bitter panicum (Figure 92), and less frequently cordgrass. When these are well established the next phase of replanting using more attractive shrubs and plants can be undertaken.

American beachgrass is available from private nurseries in the Carolinas, and has been available from state nurseries in both states.

Building a Lawn

Because grasses have greater tolerance to salt spray than other plants a beach lawn is not quite the task one might think. It is more challenging in some ways than a conventional lawn, but the results can be just as pleasing to the eye and as attractive a part of the landscape scene as are lawns grown under less arduous conditions.

We have mentioned the need to enrich the sand associated with the usual beach home. On beach area lawns three grasses seem most satisfactory. They are centipede grass (Figure 93), St. Augustine

90. *Persea borbonia,* redbay (Photo courtesy Soil Conservation Service)

91. *Ammophila breviligulata,* American beachgrass (Photo courtesy Soil Conservation Service)

92. *Panicum amarum,* bitter panicum (Photo courtesy Soil Conservation Service)

or Charleston grass, and Bermuda grass (Figure 94). Centipede and Bermuda are by far the most commonly used in the Carolinas. All of these are warm-season grasses, brown in the winter months and bright green in the summer months.

Centipede, St. Augustine, and Bermuda grass are established by vegetative propagations by "sprigging," the use of parts of the plant buried partway into the lawn area. As they grow they fill in the vacant spaces until with some modest luck a green lawn is to be seen.

PLANTS FOR REVEGETATION OF SANDS

GRASSES

Ammophila breviligulata, American beachgrass
A perennial growing to 2 feet in height with leaves that remain partly green in the winter. It is resistant to salt spray and is rec-

93. Centipede grass (Photo courtesy Soil Conservation Service)

94. Bermuda grass (Photo courtesy Soil Conservation Service)

ommended for marching dune zones. Because it begins to die as the sand becomes stable, other plants are usually interplanted.

Plants are dug from November to April and separated with one to three stems each, and are planted 8 inches deep about 2 feet apart.

Andropogon bittoralis, seacoast bluestem

A blue-colored grass growing to 1½ feet in height, covered with silvery, short hairs. Propagation can be with seeds planted in the sand dunes, as well as by chopping old stems into the ground.

Elymus virginicus 'Globriflorus,' longawn, Virginia wild rye

A cool-season grass that does better in moist areas, although it will grow in the dunes. The seed should be planted from July to September.

Muhlenbergia capillaris, hairawn muhly

Growing from 2–3 feet in height, this bunchgrass is useful for dunes, as a border or salt-wind barrier.

Panicum amarulum, panicgrass

A dense bunchgrass which grows to 4 feet in height and is excellent for sand dunes. The clumps of plants should be dug and divided, then planted a foot apart, as a border or salt-wind barrier.

Panicum amarum, bitter panicum

A low-growing, wide-spreading variety adapted for the initial planting. The plants are dug and rhizomes are cut into 1-foot lengths, with two nodes each for planting, about 4–8 feet apart, in early spring. A teaspoon of complete fertilizer, 5–10–5, after beginning spring growth is recommended for each plant.

Paspalum vaginatum, seashore paspalum

Not suitable for dry sand areas, it is useful in the high-tide water area where flooding is frequent. It is planted by dividing the plants and planting the runners and rhizomes.

Spartina patens, marshbay cordgrass

A grass growing from 2–2½ feet in height that does well both in dunes and in moist areas but requires adequate moisture. It is suggested for use in barren moist flats, channel banks, and ditches. The plants are propagated by means of sections of rhizomes with several stems rooted at the base cut up for planting 3 feet apart and 4 inches deep. Each plant should receive about a teaspoon of complete fertilizer, 5–10–5, during early summer.

Uniola paniculata, sea oats

A grass with stems to 3 feet in height that is considered the most important in the initial period of planting. Slower-growing varieties are suggested since the others tend to grow in mounds, leaving the sides and slopes unprotected.

The digging of wild sea oats and the cutting of wild seed heads is illegal in the Carolinas, so the gardener will have to get propagating materials from someone who has this plant growing on private land. The stock is planted a foot deep, and watered in early spring. It may be planted 4 to 8 feet apart. Seeds in the nursery are gathered when ripe and are planted 2–3 inches deep during the dormant season.

HERBACEOUS PLANTS

Commelina erecta, day flower

This relative of the wandering Jew (zebrina), which has stems to 3 feet in height, is good for sand dunes. It has light blue flowers and grass-like leaves and is grown from summer cuttings, or by dividing the plants.

Croton punctatus, silver-leaf croton

An annual with silvery foliage covered with soft hairs. The seed can be planted from fall to March, 1–1½ inches deep. The plant will usually reseed itself after the first year.

Hydrocotyle bonariensis, large-leaf pennywort

A herbaceous creeper growing to 6 inches in height, this pennywort is resistant to salt spray. Recommended for dunes at a planting distance of 10 feet. Must be watched as it may spread and take over the planted areas.

Indigofera pseudo-tinctoria, false anil indigo

A perennial growing to 2 feet in height and recommended for

sand dunes. For ground cover it should be spaced 2×4 feet, and for mass planting 1½ ×1½ feet.

Iva imbricata, elder

A perennial which grows to 3½ feet in height, with salt-spray-resistant foliage. It grows on beaches along the high-tide mark, and can be used to build a screen to protect other plants from salt spray.

Santolina chamaecyparissus, cypress lavender cotton

A branched silver-gray evergreen growing to 2 feet in height, noted for its aromatic leaves and yellow flowers. It is very resistant to salt spray, thrives on dry, poor soil, and will die if overwatered or overfertilized. It is recommended for borders, rock gardens, and around shrubs or trees as a filler.

Smilax auriculata, wild bamboo

A vine that grows in the shape of a shrub, is very resistant to salt spray, and grows well on sand. It can be used as a windscreen when grown on a fence or trellis, and as a ground cover on the dunes.

Solidago sempervirens, seaside goldenrod

A typical goldenrod with yellow flowers appearing around October adds an unusually healthy touch of yellow and green to the sand. It is propagated by rhizomes.

Strophostyles helvola, trailing wild bean

An annual with rose-lavender legume-type flowers that forms a very dense trailing plant. It is grown from seeds planted during the dormant season 2 inches deep, which germinate in the spring.

Vitis aestivalis, summer grape, pigeon grape

A native southern grape that can cover the ground and shrubbery and vegetation around it. It withstands salt spray and grows well in the sand. Recommended for trellises and fences, it may be a little coarse and open for a ground cover.

Vitis rotundifolia, muscadine grape

Another native southern grape, which grows well in the sand and is fairly resistant to salt spray. It is usually planted behind a barrier of shrubs or trees for protection; as a ground cover for the sand dunes it can be planted about 4 feet apart and will grow flat on the ground. It can be grown on trellises, fences, and arbors.

RECOMMENDED REFERENCES

Graetz, Karl E. *Seacoast Plants of the Carolinas for Conservation and Beautification.* U. S. Department of Agriculture, Soil Conservation Service, Raleigh, N.C., and Columbia, S.C., February 1973.

North Carolina Agricultural Extension Service, *Plants for Seaside Conditions.* Horticultural Information Leaflet No. 502. North Carolina State University, Raleigh, N.C. 27607, October 1963.

CHAPTER 15
Mobile Homes

Mobile homes seemingly are increasing in numbers every day. For many families they represent a long-term investment and are semi-permanent.

Individual mobile homes in a rural setting or on a sizable lot can be treated as a smaller home, for gardens and plants. Mobile homes in closer quarters, such as a park, require special consideration to provide privacy, an indication of use, and "ownership" boundaries.

The Problem

Mobile home lots are small, averaging between 1,500 to 2,500 square feet, about one fifth as large as private home lots. Another problem arises from the fact that the mobile homes are perpendicular to the street 70 to 95 per cent of the time, as compared to the almost universal parallel orientation of subdivision homes. These points are involved in establishing a garden program.

Important also is the rental basis of mobile home tenancy, which does not provide much incentive for establishing permanent plantings. It is hard to think of a transient tenant improving someone else's property under ordinary circumstances. The possibility under some circumstances could be improvement by a cooperative program, in which long-term tenants provide the labor for planting and the owner provides the plants, a system often used with painting of rental properties.

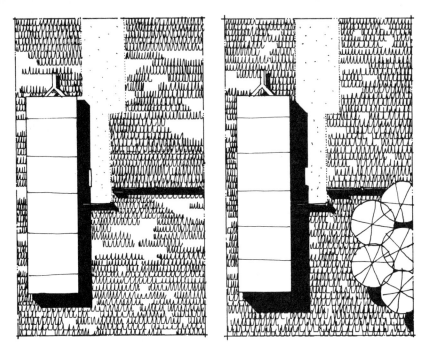

95. Left: This sketch demonstrates two approaches to simple landscaping of mobile homes. There is a simple fence for privacy which also creates a front yard and back yard. Lawn has been planted. Right: The same as the sketch on the left with the addition of some trees to mark out more clearly lines between properties or yards. (Sketch by Mike Moose)

Area Definition

If conditions are conducive to gardening as a means of increasing the resident's feeling of privacy and domain, as well as contributing to the attractiveness of the home, consideration should be given to definition of areas.

Because the front of a trailer defined by the entranceway is generally on its side, and not toward the street, a front yard is hard to define.

A beginning can be made with the establishment of a lawn, and some sort of screening, of fencing perhaps, near the trailer entrance (Figure 95). As time and plants permit, a row of plants such as box-wood, honeysuckle, roses, or similar shrubs can be planted in front of the screen, which itself serves to establish "front" and "back" yards.

The principal requirements in selecting plants, all of which should be shrubs for the purposes listed above, are slow growth to a modest height of 2 to 6 feet, evergreen for year-round color. The same concern for proper selection as to light requirements should be considered.

Lawns are usually too small to be of much concern; an annual garden with some bulbs can be set out in some unused area.

For base plantings plants should be set about 3 to 4 feet from the trailer to allow for growth.

RECOMMENDED PLANTS

Abelia spp., dwarf abelia
Grows in all areas. See Chapter 6.

Aucuba japonica, aucuba, gold-dust
Grows in the Appalachian mountains and the Piedmont plateau. See Chapter 6.

Gardenia jasminoides, and *G. thunbergia,* cape jasmine
Grows in all areas. See Chapter 6.

Ilex crenata, Japanese holly
Grows in all areas. See Chapter 6.

Juniperus conferta, shore juniper
Grows in all areas.

Myrica cerifera, wax myrtle
Grows in the Piedmont plateau and the coastal plains. See Chapter 6.

Evergreen Shrubs for Screening
 Buxus sempervirens, boxwood
 See Chapter 6.
 Camellia japonica, camellia
Grows in the Piedmont plateau and the coastal plain. See Chapter 6.
 Ilex cornuta, Chinese holly
Grows in all regions. See Chapter 6.

Juniperus chinensis, 'Spaeth,' and *J. pfitzeriana,* Pfitzer juniper
See Chapter 6.
Rhododendron spp., rhododendron
See Chapter 6.
Viburnum spp., viburnum
See Chapter 6.

RECOMMENDED REFERENCES

North Carolina Agricultural Extension Service, *Mobile Home Landscape.* Horticultural Information Leaflet No. 523, North Carolina State University, Raleigh, N.C. 27607.

CHAPTER 16

Wild Plants for Gardens

Native plants can add a great deal to a garden, bringing a touch of the field and the forest to one's own turf.

The great danger is that some of our dwindling populations of wild plants may be threatened by overenthusiastic gardeners. Sites of new roads and areas being destroyed during development are excellent sources of native plants, and contractors and realtors usually will permit removal of plants ahead of the bulldozer. Nurseries in the Carolinas often have these plants in stock.

Seeds, fruits, and cuttings can be collected for propagation where permitted, without threatening the survival of wild plants; plants themselves never should be collected, unless as indicated above.

The North Carolina Botanical Garden at Chapel Hill has a superb collection of native plants on continuous display. Visits there would provide the gardener an opportunity to see what the plants look like in a partially cultivated setting during different seasons of the year. Because so many kinds are on display, an unlimited number of field trips to see native plants in the field can be condensed into fewer visits to Chapel Hill.

The display includes species easy to cultivate as landscape plants or container plants, which are readily propagated by seeds or cuttings.

WILD PERENNIALS

Aristida stricta, wire grass

A perennial grass found in the Piedmont plateau and the coastal plains of both Carolinas. It prefers a sandy location and is suited for specimen plantings, and possibly borders. Propagation by root.

Aster grandiflorus, blue aster

Found in North Carolina in the coastal plain and the Piedmont plateau growing to 2½ feet in height. It will grow on poor soil, including pinelands, and grows in full sun or partial shade. It is a perennial with purple flowers. It is adapted to use in borders, mass plantings, and for cut flowers. Propagated by seed.

Aster pilosus, frost aster

A perennial that is found in regions of the Carolinas. It is a white aster that will grow in sun or partial shade, in poor and neutral soil. It varies greatly in size between 1 and 6 feet. It can be tried in borders or small groups, and for cut flowers. Propagated by seed.

Bidens aristosa, tickweed

An annual 2 to 3 feet in height with large yellow flowers to 3 inches across. Many other species are found in both states. It tolerates sun and partial shade and grows in moist areas. It is suggested as a specimen and for cut flowers.

Coreopsis helianthoides, coreopsis

Found in the coastal plain of North Carolina in alluvial woods and swamps. It prefers neutral soil and shade and damp areas. A smooth perennial growing from 18 inches to 6 feet in height, it has reddish flowers. It can be propagated by basal offshoots or rhizomes.

Cyperus strigosus, sedge

A perennial found in coastal plain and Piedmont of the Carolinas. It is a yellowish-green sedge that prefers moist areas. It lacks the joints that most grasses have. It is recommended for growing in containers. Propagated by seed.

96. *Drosera capillaris*, sundew (Photo by Charles Balducci)

Dichromena latifolia, white bracted sedge, sandswamp sedge

Found in the coastal plain of the Carolinas. It is a plant that prefers wet locations, is adapted to sun and partial shade and grows to 2 feet in height. The star-like bracts are attractive even after blooming. Blooms May to September and can be propagated by seeds and rhizomes.

Dioscorea batatas, cinnamon vine, Chinese yam

D. batatas does well in the Piedmont plateau and the Appalachian mountains and may be tried on the coastal plain. It is excellent along a fence or in containers. The small potato-like tubers that grow in the leaf axils should be planted about 3 inches deep in sandy loam with support for the vines. They are planted in the fall and need mulching over winter.

Drosera capillaris, sundew (Figure 96)

This native of the coastal plains is a low, spreading perennial with leaves to ½ inch in length which rest directly on the ground. The spines clustered on the end of the leaves are tipped with a sticky, clear fluid which traps insects. The fluid reflects in the sun somewhat like dew, and thus the name sundew. It prefers rather moist, sandy, well-drained places. It propagates by seed. It is excellent as borders around other plants, in rock gardens. It is best used in great numbers, and away from other plants, as its size will handicap it otherwise. It should not be collected in the wild, but propagated or bought in nurseries.

Eryngium integrifolium, eryngium
This plant grows from the Appalachian mountains to the coastal plains, usually in wet areas. The flowers are blue. The plant, a perennial, is somewhat shorter than *E. yuccifolium.*

Eryngium yuccifolium, button snakeroot, rattlesnake master
A perennial that grows in all regions in both dry and moist areas, and is common along roadsides. The flowers are either blue or white, the foliage resembles that of yucca, and the plant may grow to 6 feet in height. Will grow in sand or clay soils, in partial shade and sun. Suited for borders, along fences, and as specimens.

Hexastylis arifolia, heart leaf
An evergreen which grows in all regions in moist or dry locations. Propagated by rhizomes, and grows to 8 inches in height. Ground cover.

Hexastylis virginica, wild ginger
This plant grows in all regions in shaded forests and rocky hills and prefers shaded locations with adequate drainage. It grows to 8 inches in height and can be propagated by rhizomes. Ground cover.

Juncus coriaceus, juncus
Juncus grows in the Piedmont and the coastal plain in wet locations to a height of 1½ feet. It can be propagated by seed and is suited for use as a ground cover in low, wet, shaded areas.

Liatris spicata, blazing star
This plant grows in the Appalachian mountains and prefers a moist

location. The flowers are a rose-purple. It can be propagated from seed and grows to 6 feet in height, and will grow in shade and partial shade.

Ludwigia alternifolia, seedbox

Seedbox grows in all regions, usually in damp, shady areas. The yellow flowers produce fruit capsules and a striking fall color. It grows to a height of 4 feet.

Sarracenia minor, hooded pitcherplant (Figure 97)

An insectivorous plant which prefers a wet location and can be grown from seed, *S. minor* is found in areas of the coastal plain. It grows in the sun or shade and prefers damp, peaty soil. Related species are found mostly along the coast, but also in the Piedmont and a few in the mountains.

97. *Sarracenia minor,* pitcherplant (Photo by Arnold Krochmal)

Solidago spp., goldenrod

These perennials bloom in late summer and fall, grow to 6 feet in height, and can be found in all parts of the Carolinas. They are adapted to a range of soils and light conditions. Most of the species can be propagated by rhizomes or seed. The shorter species are suited for mass plantings, the taller for specimen plantings.

Tiarella cordifolia, foamflower

Foamflower grows in the Piedmont plateau and the Appalachian mountains to 18 inches in height with white flowers. The heart-shaped leaves, 2 to 4 inches long, remain on the plant over winter. It prefers a moist soil in a shady area. It can be propagated by rhizomes. It can be used in mass plantings and for cut flowers. Perennial.

Xanthorhiza simplicissima, yellow-root

This plant is a shrubby perennial found in all regions, growing to 2 feet in height. The wood is bright yellow. It can be propagated from seed and suckers. It is suited for very wet areas, in partial shade.

WILD SHRUBS

Callicarpa americana, beauty-berry

Adapted to seashore areas, this shrub is considered drought-resistant and does well on poor soil in sun and partial shade. It has bright lavender berries. It is propagated by fall planting of the seed or by cuttings in September. The stems should be cut to the ground in the spring to promote new growth.

Chionanthus virginicus, fringe tree, old-man's-beard

This plant does well in all regions. Its lacy, white, fragrant flowers appear in June and are a favorite. It is either a small tree or a large shrub, and prefers partial shade and dry areas. It is a good specimen and shade tree and is propagated by seed.

Clethra alnifolia, sweet pepper bush

Adapted to seashore use, *C. alnifolia* prefers moist, sunny areas. It forms a spreading thicket to 8 feet in height, and produces white fragrant flowers in midsummer. Another species, *C. acuminata,* is found in the higher areas of the Appalachian mountains and grows in partial shade.

Cyrilla racemiflora, titi

Adapted to the coastal plain, titi can be a tall shrub or a small tree, sometimes growing to 25 feet in height. The clusters of white flowers appear in early spring. A fine specimen plant, propagated by seed.

Euonymus americanus, strawberry bush

This plant does well in all regions in moist, sunny locations or partial shade, and grows to 5 feet in height. It has characteristic green stems with yellow-green flowers that produce red fruits in the fall. It is useful as a specimen plant and in borders.

Fothergilla major

This shrub blooms in the very early spring, with hazel-yellow flowers, and grows to 5 feet in height.

Hypericum densiflorum, St.-John's-wort

Mostly found on the coastal plain and Appalachian mountains on dry, sandy soil, growing to 6 feet in height, in partial shade to sun. The yellow flowers appear over several weeks during the summer. Adapted to dry areas, and can be grown as specimens or borders. There are several other potentially usable species found in all areas.

Kalmia angustifolia, sheep-kill, sheep laurel

This evergreen grows in the Appalachian mountains and the coastal plains, sometimes to a height of 8 feet, in dry, rocky areas as well as wet spots, with dark rose flowers. It can be propagated by cuttings and seed, and is an ideal specimen plant.

Leucothoe axillaris, leucothoe

Found in all parts of the Carolinas, this evergreen grows to 4 feet in height with dense clusters of small cream-colored flowers. It prefers a rich, moist soil and shade. It does best along the coastal plain and mountains, but is also found in the upper Piedmont. It is used in rock gardens and borders. It can be propagated by seed and cuttings.

Rhus aromatica, fragrant sumac

This plant does well in the Appalachian mountains and the Piedmont plateau, on rocky soils in sun, and grows to 6 feet in height. Its small yellow flowers appear in spring, giving rise to compact red fruits. Propagated by seed and used as a specimen.

Rhus copallina, smooth sumac, dwarf sumac (Figure 98)

This shrub or tree of the Appalachian mountains and the Pied-

98. *Rhus* spp., sumac (Photo courtesy U. S. Forest Service)

mont grows to 20 feet. It does well in dry, sterile conditions in the sun, and provides colorful fruit and foliage from summer through fall. May be propagated by rhizomes and seeds. An attractive specimen plant.

Stewartia ovata, mountain camellia

Found mainly in the Appalachian mountains as a shrub growing to 15 feet in height, with white flowers up to 3 inches across. In the fall the shrub has attractive orange or red foliage. Prefers moist soils, partial shade. Propagated by seed.

Symphoricarpos orbiculatus, coralberry, Indian currant

Coralberry does well in the Appalachian mountains and the Piedmont plateau, growing to 6 feet in height. It prefers a neutral soil but does well in a variety of locations. It bears a red berry which often remains on the tree over winter. It is a good specimen, hedge, and border plant and is propagated by seed.

Symplocos tinctoria, horse sugar, sweetleaf

A shrub or small tree growing to 20 feet in height which holds its leaves until spring, following masses of light, fragrant, yellow flowers. Generally found in the Appalachian mountains and coastal plain. A handsome specimen propagated by seeds.

Vaccinium corymbosum, highbush blueberry

This plant does well in the Piedmont plateau and the coastal plains, growing to 15 feet in height in wet or dry locations on acid soil in partial shade. It provides red foliage in the fall and red twigs in the winter. The blue berries are edible and this plant is the ancestor of cultivated blueberries. It is propagated by seed and used as a specimen or for massed planting.

Vaccinium erythrocarpum, mountain cranberry, and *V. macrocarpum,*
    cranberry

Both are found in the Appalachian mountains. Mountain cranberry is also found in the bogs and woodlands. It has red flowers. Cranberry is a creeper and makes a good ground cover. It has white to rose flowers.

NATIVE PALMS

Native palms can be grown in the coastal plain and lower elevations of the Piedmont plateau.

To transplant specimens, a very large hole is needed, partially refilled with rotted leaves, compost, or other organic material.

Summer is best for planting. Plants should be moved with a ball of earth. Regular watering is a must for at least the first year.

Palms can be used for specimens and along driveways on large properties.

Sabal minor, blue-stem palmetto

This stemless low shrub produces fan-shaped leaves up to 3 feet across. The leafstalks are smooth and have a bluish appearance. It is a native of the coastal plain and can be found in wet woods.

99. *Sabal palmetto,* cabbage palmetto (Photo courtesy U. S. Forest Service)

Sabal palmetto, cabbage palmetto (Figure 99)

This tree, growing to 40 feet in height, has fan-shaped leaves, dark green and shiny, which may be as long as 5 feet and as wide as 5 feet. It is a native of the coastal plain and is found in the marshes and forests near the sea.

FERNS

Ferns can be used as ground covers and under trees in low spots. Low damp, shady areas are ideal for ferns. We have a handsome Christmas fern in a low spot in our garden that flourishes, even after being heavily inundated in an unexpected spring flood.

Although ferns reproduce by spores, the small brown nodules on the underside of the leaves, it is far easier for most gardeners to transfer the entire plant with a ball of earth.

Adiantum pedatum, maidenhair fern (Figure 100)

Native to the Appalachian mountains and the Piedmont plateau, this graceful fern prefers rich, shaded, humid areas.

Asplenium platyneuron, ebony spleenwort

This evergreen fern grows in all regions. It prefers partial shade in rocky areas or sandy pinelands, but will grow also in full sunlight.

Athryium asplenioides, southern lady fern

This delicate fern is distinguished by a reddish fringe on the leafstalks. It is found in all regions in swamps, meadows, and forests, and is easily transplanted.

Onoclea sensibilis, sensitive fern

Medium green and stoutly branched, this marsh dweller will tolerate dry spells, shade, and some sun at higher elevations. It occurs in all parts of the Carolinas.

Osmunda cinnamomea, cinnamon fern

This fern grows in all regions. The most sun-tolerant fern in the Carolinas, it turns a rich brown in the fall. It will grow in full sun or shade in moist locations.

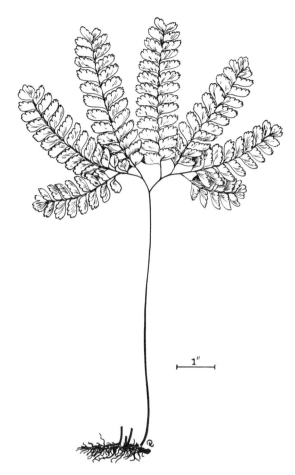

100. *Adiantum pedatum,* maidenhair fern (Courtesy U. S. Forest Service)

Polystichum acrostichoides, Christmas fern

Christmas fern grows in all regions. A very popular garden plant and easy to grow, this dark green fern thrives in semi- to heavy shade and moist but well-drained areas. It has a hairy, shedding leafstalk. It is good for containers.

Thelypteris normalis, shield fern

Shield fern grows in the coastal plain in South Carolina. When taken from its natural habitat of alkaline soil and planted in potting soil, it will reach several times its natural size.

Thelypteris palustris, marsh fern
This fern grows in all regions, in wet, low, shady locations.

Woodwardia areolata, netted chain fern
W. areolata grows in all regions. Some leaves are green while others are a shiny purple-brown. It grows in bogs, wet forests, and acid swamps in shady areas.

RECOMMENDED REFERENCES

Justice, William S., and C. Ritchie Bell. *Wild Flowers of North Carolina.* Chapel Hill, University of North Carolina Press, 1968.

CHAPTER 17

Diseases

Plant diseases can be destructive if left unchecked, and can ruin the efforts of the gardener. A basic knowledge of the symptoms and principles of control of the more important classes of diseases can help in keeping the garden area healthy and attractive.

Because there are so many diseases that can be found on lawns, shrubs, annuals, perennials, and trees we will touch only on the highlights. The three principal disease causes are fungi, bacteria, and viruses. Both Clemson and North Carolina State have illustrated leaflets covering the range of diseases of garden plants.

FUNGUS DISEASES

Fungi exist in the soil on plants and the spores are often found in the air. Invasion by fungi takes place through stomates and other natural openings in plants; through wounds and damaged places; and sometimes by direct invasion of the plant surface.

Insects may transmit fungi by carrying disease organisms, and in a secondary way by wounding tissues, permitting entrance of the fungi. Nematodes, or eelworms, the damaging soil organisms that feed on plant roots, are often responsible for providing damaged spots permitting entry of soil fungi.

Nutritional deficiencies can result in chlorotic symptoms, leaf burning, and reduced growth which can be confused with parasitic diseases. If your soil has been tested and you maintain a reasonable fertility program, chances of deficiencies are relatively small.

Mildews. Downy mildew may be found on any of the above-ground plant parts; there is usually a light tan or grayish patch, which turns brown as it enlarges.

Powdery mildew may also be found on aboveground parts in the form of a gray to white powdery covering. The spots can grow together to form a large yellow area. Both mildews can be found on almost all ornamentals.

Leaf spots. These are the most common of garden diseases (Figure 101) and generally not serious. Many of the spots have concentric lines, but differ in size, shape, and color. Sometimes the center of the spot drops out, leaving a shot-hole effect.

Rusts are more often a pest of evergreens, appearing as yellow, orange, brown, or black swellings on stems and leaves. Many rusts require a second plant other than the host evergreen to complete the life cycle.

Smuts may appear on all parts of a plant from bulbs to seeds. The symptoms include very dark brown powdery masses inside light-colored blisters.

Wilts are often indicated by reduced growth, yellowing of leaves, and wilting of the plant. If the stem is cut lengthwise and examined the inside will appear streaked and darkly discolored.

Damping off. One of the greatest problems in growing young plants, which display symptoms above the soil line, in a pinching or constricting effect, usually dark brown. The plants fall over.

Root rots are widespread and rather difficult to diagnose because the symptoms are underground and a number of diseases resemble each other. If young plants fall over and examination of the roots reveal molds of different colors, a fungus root rot is probably at work.

VIRUS DISEASES

Mosaic, color break, and *leaf curl* are difficult to diagnose because the symptoms are easily confused with those of nutrient deficiency. Leaves and flowers with mosaic appear mottled with light and dark green blotches and are stunted.

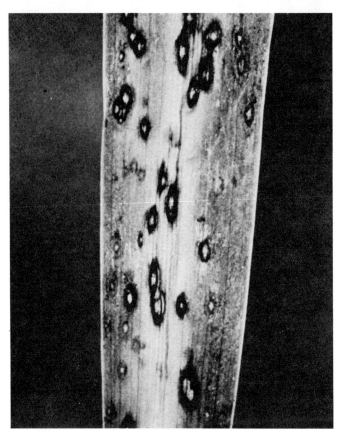

101. Iris leaf spot (Photo courtesy Clemson University Cooperative Extension Service)

Malforming and twisting of leaves and flowers and puckering of the leaf borders are also symptomatic of virus diseases.

Yellowing can result in a marked chlorosis or yellowing of an entire plant. *Rosetting,* a tight, compact growth of leaves and shoots, is symptomatic of another virus.

Viruses are usually introduced into plants by insects, often by aphids and less often by leaf hoppers, thrips, and mites. Other insects can serve as vectors but do so very rarely.

A few viruses are carried on seeds. Sometimes grafting and vegetative propagation can transmit a virus from a diseased plant to a healthy one. Infected cuttings, bulbs, corms, rhizomes, and tubers can be guilty of transmitting viruses. However, it is almost impossible to identify viral infections on underground propagating materials.

BACTERIAL DISEASES

Bacteria are single-celled organisms which form colonies varying in shape. They attack internal and external areas of plants, by way of the leaf openings or stomates, and wounds. They are not as troublesome as fungi and viruses.

Some bacteria grow rapidly enough to clog conducting tissues, resulting in wilting and death. Others can cause very visible galls (Figure 102) on different plant parts, and some cause spots and subsequent decay.

Bacteria prefer warm climates, making the Carolinas an ideal location for their development. They do not send out strands, as do fungi; they move as units of one or more cells, going from plant to plant via insects, raindrops, and infected plants parts.

102. Azalea leaf gall (Photo courtesy Clemson University Cooperative Extension Service)

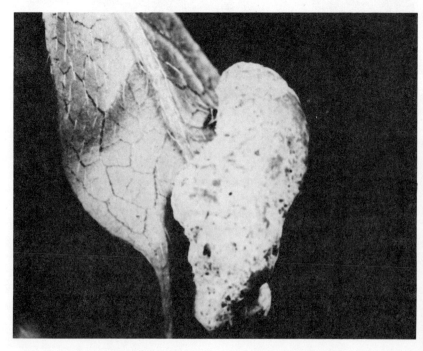

Symptoms of bacterial diseases can easily be confused with those of fungi and viruses. The most common symptoms of bacterial invasion are the presence of swellings and enlargement of plant areas, and death of tissue.

Bacteria have an ability to live over winter in diseased plants and plant residues, as well as in the bark of woody plants, and in lesions.

Wilts, rots, blights are difficult to identify because the symptoms are changeable. Water-soaked spots, shriveled stems, and sudden wilting are seen. Sometimes foliage turns greenish-gray, then brown. The stem rots at the ground and separates easily from the roots.

103. Fire blight of tulip (Photo courtesy Clemson University Cooperative Extension Service)

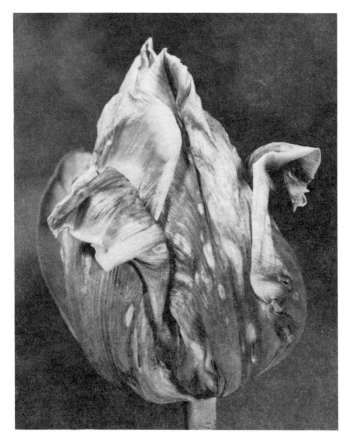

Cankers, dieback are produced by fungi as well as bacteria, and the gardener will be hard put to distinguish which is which. Some cankers are soft, others hard, and the size range extends from a baseball or larger down to a pea.

Shoot blight, fire blight (Figure 103). Once cankers of this bacteria become established, they serve as a source of infection, and bacteria are washed by rainfall to other plants, carried by insects and sometimes by garden implements. All of the plant parts will suddenly become dark brown and shriveled as if damaged by fire.

Bacterial rot is indicated when a smelly, watery splotching appears on any part of the plant, above or below the ground.

Crown gall is a frequent disease in nurseries and is symptomized by large galls at ground level or near a graft or bud union.

DISEASE CONTROL

The basic step in controlling an existing disease is the proper identification of the problem. Experience, plus leaflets available from the state extension programs, will be indispensable. The services of the state diagnostic laboratories in severe cases can be of real value.

Sanitation

Initially the practice of control measures depends largely on good judgment and common sense. One of the practical means of controlling the spread of disease is the removal and disposal of diseased plants and plant parts.

We have had a problem for two years of dogwoods dying. One trunk of a clump in several areas died from an unknown disease.

We cut out the dead trunks for firewood, removing a focus of infection and adding to our firewood supply. The surviving trunks, fertilized and watered, have all grown well, with the infection eliminated.

Proper drainage, which we have discussed in other parts of this book, is a critical factor in controlling rots and disease. If seedbed preparation has been done with care, this problem should not arise.

Pest control, whether weeds or insects, is another basic sanitation measure to be followed. Weeds can act as hosts for a range of viruses and for fungal and bacterial diseases. Insects can transmit disease from infected weeds to garden plants.

We do not use chemical herbicides ourselves but a number are available which, with care, can help control weeds on lawns. Elsewhere a hoe or another implement or hand picking serves well.

Select for storage only healthy and clean tubers, bulbs, and corms and destroy any with signs of disease or insects.

Chemical Control

Fungus treatments can be divided into two classes, preventative and curative. Preventative materials are protectants and act to kill the fungus before it can invade the plant. These materials can be used on seed and in soil applications. Used as dusts or sprays they are more effective when applied before periods of wetness.

Protective fungicide, used to kill fungi which have become established in a plant, are used as dusts or sprays on foliage and seeds and in the soil. In some cases the same chemical can be used at differing concentrations to serve both purposes.

Virus diseases are not amenable to chemical treatment. The elimination of diseased plants may be necessary. Control of insect vectors is not too practical for the home gardener because such vectors would be moving in from elsewhere rather rapidly.

Bacterial diseases. The home gardener's best defense against bacterial diseases is sanitation, the destroying of infected plants. Any garden tools that may have been in contact with diseased plants should be cleaned with a disinfectant. Resistance to bacterial diseases is bred into agricultural crops, but is not too common in ornamentals.

Applying Chemicals

A perennial discussion focuses on whether dusting or spraying is most effective. Generally we personally prefer sprays because there is less drifting of the chemical and less inhalation when we spray (Figure 104).

Dusts, in combination for insects and diseases, sold as rose dusts, for example, are available and quite convenient, requiring no additional equipment to apply.

Sprays last longer on foliage than do dusts, are considered to be more effective, and leave no visible covering on the foliage.

The choice of equipment for dusting and spraying is wide. The size of the area to be treated will of course determine the size of the equipment that is bought. Sprayers should be cleaned with soapy water after use, and allowed to drain.

Because of changing products on the market, and concern with chemical sprays, we are omitting specific control recommendations, suggesting these are best obtained from North Carolina State and Clemson Extension personnel, who are in touch with newest practices.

LAWN DISEASES

Diseases on lawn grass display marked symptoms when the disease has become a real problem. It is almost impossible to notice a few ailing blades of grass. The major lawn grass diseases are fungal in origin.

Sometimes disease "symptoms" are not really signs of diseases at all. Stray dogs urinating on a lawn can cause browning and death of patches of grass. Overfertilization can cause burning and streaking.

Mowing too close, or too often, can cause damage and browning. Kentucky bluegrass, red fescue, and other upright grasses should be mowed to a height of 2 inches. Once the growing season has begun do not lower the cutting height. Clippings can be left in place, a practice we ourselves follow because it returns organic matter and minerals to the soil.

FUNGI

Fungi are quite often visible to the naked eye, presenting an appearance of a mass of threads in a range of colors. Some fungus diseases appear as round spots, often as concentric circles. Other fungus diseases appear on blades as dead spots, with an inner circle falling out, creating a shot-hole effect.

Dollar spot or *small brown patch* is most prevalent during early spring and late fall, when nitrogen is deficient. Bleached spots, the size of a silver dollar, are the first symptoms. These spots may merge to form irregular patches of dead grass.

Rust. Heavy moisture favors the appearance of this fungus, usually in late summer. Diseased grass blades become covered with yellow to orange blisters. Walking through a rust-infested lawn can leave shoes with a coating of orange. Frequent mowing may help.

104. Proper spraying procedure (Photo courtesy U. S. Department of Agriculture)

Leaf spot or *fading out* is extremely destructive and attacks fescue, Kentucky bluegrass, and bentgrass. The disease is prevalent from May to October during periods of high humidity.

Reddish-brown spots with light-colored centers are found on the blades, which then shrivel and die. Eventually the entire plant dies.

Brown patch attacks most grass species grown in the Carolinas during warm, humid weather. It is likely to appear on lawns which have been overfertilized with nitrogen. It differs from small brown patch in having irregular circular areas a few inches to several feet in diameter with a brownish discoloration. The dead grass remains erect and does not fall over. In the early morning while the grass is wet with dew, white tufts of the fungus on the blades may be seen. Sometimes heavy strips of grass cuttings may precipitate the disease. New grass often covers the attacked areas.

Pythium blight is particularly troublesome in poorly drained areas. The symptom most commonly seen is a spot or group of spots about 2 inches in diameter surrounded by blackened leaf blades covered with fungus threads. Diseased leaves become water-soaked and slimy, ultimately drying up and browning. The grass appears to lie flat as compared to the erect appearance of brown patch.

Fairy rings are the symptoms of mushrooms growing on a lawn. The rings formed are dark green with an inner circle of dying, brown grass. The green area is where the mushrooms have been growing.

Slime molds appear as dark brown or black blobs on leaf blades. The damage done is not too serious other than resulting in a discoloration of the leaf blades. During a dry spell the mold will dry up and disappear. Raking, hosing, or the use of a broom will eliminate the unsightly masses.

RECOMMENDED REFERENCES

Clemson University Extension Service, *Insects and Diseases of Ornamentals: How to Control Them.* Circular 502, Clemson University, Clemson, S.C. 29631, February 1972.

Department of Pathology, *Damping Off in Seed Beds, Flower and Vegetable Seedlings.* Plant Pathology Information Note 69, North Carolina State University, Raleigh, N.C. 27607, June 1972.

Heald, Frederick Deforest. *Introduction to Plant Pathology.* McGraw-Hill, New York, 1937.

North Carolina Agricultural Extension Service, *Broad Leaved Weed Control with 2,4-D.* Horticultural Leaflet No. 504, North Carolina State University, Raleigh, N.C. 27607, October 1965.

————, *Grass Control with Dalapon.* Horticultural Information Leaflet No. 508, North Carolina State University, Raleigh, N.C. 27607, October 1965.

————, *Pythium Root and Stem Diseases of Chrysanthemum in North Carolina.* Technical Bulletin No. 158, North Carolina State University, Raleigh, N.C. 27607, January 1964.

Shurtleff, Malcolm C. *How to Control Plant Diseases.* Iowa State University Press, Ames, Iowa, 1962.

Tarr, S. A. J. *The Principles of Plant Pathology.* Winchester Press, New York, 1972.

U. S. Department of Agriculture, *Milky Disease for Control of Japanese Beetle Grubs.* Leaflet No. 500, Washington, D.C. 20250, December 1961.

CHAPTER 18

Insects[1]

Thousands upon thousands of species of insects occur in the Carolinas. Many are harmful to ornamental plants. However, gardeners often become unduly alarmed at the presence of insects which do not harm; this could be easily remedied with a little foreknowledge.

Plant-feeding insects can be grouped into two broad classes: those with chewing mouthparts and those with sucking mouthparts. In general, pesticides which are effective against one chewing insect will control others (exceptions exist, a few of which are mentioned below) and likewise for sucking insects. Advice about which pesticides to use can usually be obtained from your local garden center, county agent, or by contacting the extension entomologists at Clemson or North Carolina State universities.

SUCKING INSECTS

Aphids are the most commonly encountered sucking insects (Figure 105). They are recognized by their small size and habit of feeding in groups on the stems and buds of roses, flowering quince, crape myrtles, lilies, and many other flowering plants. They secrete a sugary liquid called honeydew on which sooty mold, a black

[1] This chapter contributed by J. R. Baker, Extension Entomologist, North Carolina State University, Raleigh, N.C.

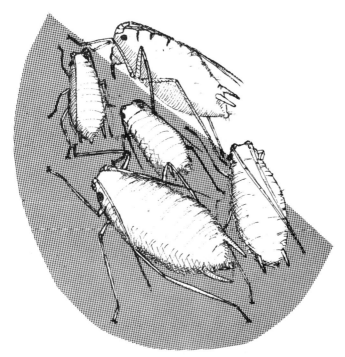

105. Many aphids feed in groups. Color may range from pale green to brown or black. (Courtesy North Carolina Agricultural Extension Service)

fungus, grows. Aphids may be tended by ants, which protect the aphids and feed on their honeydew. Aphids may be winged or wingless.

Fuzzy sucking insects, such as the woolly alder aphid found on silver maple and alder, and pine bark aphids found on white pine, are relatively easy to control early in the season. Although the woolly alder aphid disfigures maple leaves and discharges quantities of honeydew, it does not usually kill even small branches. Pine bark aphids, small, woolly sucking insects, may be more damaging to pines and firs and may eventually weaken the trees to the point that bark beetles can successfully invade and kill the tree.

Scale insects (Figure 106) are another important group of sucking insects. Except for the tiny, newly hatched immature stage and winged males, scales are immobile throughout their development. A shell or scale protects them as they grow and makes control difficult. Even the eggs are laid under scale.

106. Wax scales on Chinese holly. One-fourth inch, white.
(Courtesy North Carolina Agricultural Extension Service)

Leaf hoppers are sucking insects which generally do not do much damage except occasionally to transmit a viral disease of asters and marigolds called aster yellows. Leaf hoppers are small, slender, pale green insects which congregate at lights at night, in summer, and are also abundant on plants. Sometimes they damage lawns in dry weather.

Spittlebugs are named for their immature forms which live in a frothy mass closely resembling human spittle. A few species dam-

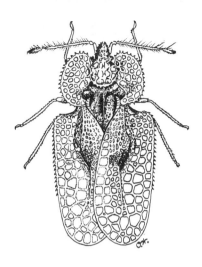

107. Lace bug (Courtesy Ohio Agricultural Extension Service)

age ornamental pines and Bermuda grass. One of the most common, the two-lined spittlebug (black with two orange lines on the wings), feeds on weeds and grasses when young and is often on hollies as adults.

Lace bugs are small sucking insects (Figure 107) which cause a noticeable mottling of plant leaves. These true bugs are usually found on azaleas, pyracanthas, oaks, sycamores, and hawthorns. Usually a species such as the azalea lace bug will attack only one plant genus, *Azalea*.

Thrips use their strange sucking-rasping mouthparts with devastating effect on white or pale roses and other pale flowers. Their feeding causes petals to curl and become mottled or an unsightly brown color. Although thrips are not difficult to control, they are often overlooked until the damage has been done because of their small size (Figure 108).

CHEWING INSECTS

Chewing insects are a more diverse lot. The more commonly encountered are beetles and caterpillars, the young stages of moths and butterflies or sawflies.

Caterpillars or *worms* are alarming but are rarely deadly to plants (Figure 109). Only the bagworm which spins a silken bag with bits

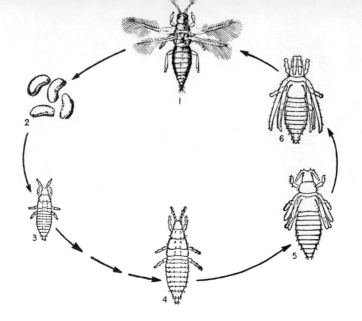

108. Life history of typical thrips: 1. Adult; 2. Eggs (inserted into plant tissue); 3. First Nymph; 4. Fourth Nymph; 5. Prepupal stage (inactive, on host plant or in soil); 6. Pupa (inactive, on host plant or in soil) (Courtesy U. S. Department of Agriculture)

of vegetation incorporated, is really dangerous to coniferous shrubs. Another caterpillar, the orange-striped oakworm, is resistant to some pesticides commonly used for worm control. However, the orange-striped oakworm is not a real threat to oaks.

Sawfly caterpillars (Figure 110) closely resemble moth young but they have more legs than moth caterpillars. The adult sawflies are wasp- or fly-like insects which are rarely seen. Sawfly worms usually feed in a group, which is convenient for control; ordinarily only a small portion of a tree or shrub need be treated.

Beetles are another group of chewing insects. They have thickened forewings (Figure 111) and usually buzz audibly as they fly. Many of the pesticides which kill caterpillars also kill leaf-feeding beetles.

The Japanese beetle is a good, or perhaps, a bad example of an insect that is damaging to ornamental plants in the immature stages as well as in the adult stage. The young are white grubs which feed on the roots of grasses—sometimes to the extent that the lawn can be rolled up like a rug! The adults feed on foliage, flowers, and fruit.

 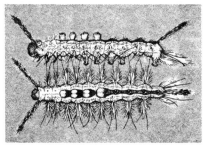

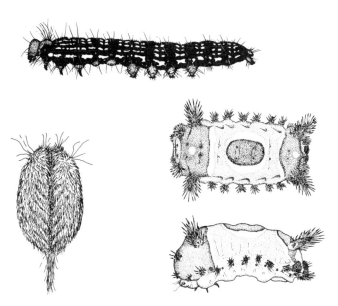

109. Leaf-feeding caterpillars; TOP, left: orange-striped oak-worm, black with yellow or orange stripes. Right: tussock moth caterpillar, brush-like tufts of hair on the back. CENTER: azalea caterpillar, black or brown with rows of yellow dots or stripes, head and legs rusty-red. BOTTOM, left: puss caterpillar, yellow to reddish-brown or gray hairs; a stinging caterpillar. Right: saddleback caterpillar, brownish, middle portion green with a brown spot on top; a stinging caterpillar. (Courtesy North Carolina Agricultural Extension Service)

To help diagnose beetle damage remember that weevils usually feed on leaf margins and other beetles usually feed on leaf surfaces. An example of a marginal-feeding weevil is the fuller rose beetle, which chews on the margins of rose and holly leaves. The young feed on roots of various ornamental plants.

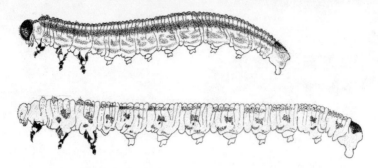

110. Leaf-feeding sawflies. Virginia pine sawfly (above) and redheaded pine sawfly (below). Adults are fly-like with two pairs of wings. Larvae resemble moth larvae except for more pairs of legs on the abdomen. Virginia pine sawfly black and gray. Redheaded pine sawfly creamy with black spots, head reddish brown. (Courtesy North Carolina Agricultural Extension Service)

LEAF MINERS

A special category of chewing insects is those which have specialized as leaf miners. Some moths, flies, sawflies, and beetles have young which are flattened for this specialized existence. Most leaf-mining young lack legs and eyes. The adult lays her eggs in the leaf, and the young form tunnels or mines as they eat their way along the leaf. Because they are between the two outer layers of the leaf, miners are difficult to control with non-systematic pesticides.

BORERS

Although trees may be protected from bark beetles by coating the trunks and large limbs with a persistent pesticide, the best control is to keep trees in vigorous health, to paint all wounds in the bark, and promptly to remove unthrifty, dying, or dead trees that could serve as a breeding place for more beetles. If a tree has fine sawdust appearing on the bark and around the base of the tree, that tree is as good as dead and should probably be removed.

Larger borer insects are difficult to control with chemicals. If limbs mysteriously die on dogwood, rhododendron, lilac, or other woody ornamentals, borers should be suspected. By feeling for soft places in the bark, one can discover their tunnels. The young can be killed with a wire inserted into the tunnels, or pried out with a knife and the wound painted with a water-based asphalt tree paint.

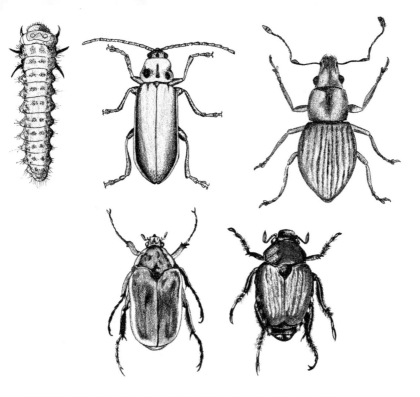

111. Leaf-feeding beetles. TOP, left: elm leaf beetle. Five-sixteenths inch long, larvae longer. Both feed on elms. Adults yellowish to dull brown. Sometimes a serious defoliator. TOP, right: Fuller rose beetle. Five-sixteenths inch long, splotchy buff on black. Adults feed on roses, hollies, other ornamental plants. BOTTOM, left: green June beetle. Three-quarters inch long, dull green with buff line at edges to wings and thorax. Feeds on wide variety of ornamental plants. BOTTOM, right: Japanese beetle. One-half inch long, shining green head, thorax and abdomen with reddish-brown wings; white spots along abdomen. Adults feed on leaves, flowers, and fruits of a wide variety of plants. (Courtesy North Carolina Agricultural Extension Service)

Twig girdlers are a special sort of borer. The mother beetle lays her eggs on twigs and small branches on pecan and other trees. She next chews around and around the branch until the branch is so weakened that it soon falls to the ground. The eggs hatch and the young bore into the now dead twig and develop into mature larvae which overwinter in the twig. Next summer the larvae emerge as adults and repeat the cycle. Many times twig girdlers are so abundant in pecan orchards that production is threatened. Gathering and burning the twigs is the best control.

GALLS

Many tiny insects and mites can cause spectacular growths on the stems and leaves of plants (Figure 112). The growths, called galls, are stimulated by the salivary secretions of the insects. These secretions mimic naturally occurring plant growth hormones. Many of these galls occur so seldomly that control is rarely needed. Galls that occur on twigs and limbs may be difficult to control with chemicals. On a small scale, pruning out twigs can help.

LAWN INSECTS

Insect pests of lawns fall into most of the previous categories. Leaf miners seem to be the only ones which do not bother lawn grasses in the Carolinas.

Grubs, the immature stages of Japanese, June, and other scarab beetles, are a principal pest of lawns. Grubs feed on grass roots as they burrow along through the soil. Development may take as long as three years, during which time many young are destroyed by predators (Figure 113), parasites, and diseases. However, even with these natural controls at work, grubs may become so numerous chemical control may be necessary.

Ants are a nuisance in the lawn because their mounds are scalped by the lawnmower. Some species may kill the roots, and other species gather seeds for food. Seed-gathering or harvester ants prevent natural reseeding.

Sod webworms make silken tubes from which they venture out to cut blades of grass. The blades are then drawn back into the tube and devoured. Numbers of sod webworms may build up unnoticed until whole patches of the lawn are devoured down to the thatch. The adults are small, dirty-gray moths which are usually overlooked as they fly along and lay their eggs in the grass.

Chinch bugs are one-eighth-inch-long sucking insects that feed on St. Augustine grass in particular. When large numbers of chinch bugs are feeding, brown patches appear in the lawn. This damage differs from sod webworm damage in that the grass is still standing but brown. With the sod webworm, the grass is clipped off and consumed.

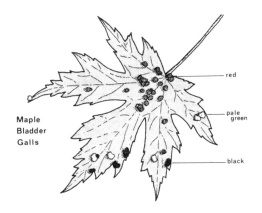

Maple
Bladder
Galls

red

pale
green

black

112. Maple bladder galls on silver maple (Courtesy North
Carolina Agricultural Extension Service)

113. Scolloid wasp, predator of beetle grubs. Bluish-black with
two yellow dots and brown-tipped abdomen. (Courtesy North
Carolina Agricultural Extension Service)

MISCELLANEOUS PESTS

Slugs and *snails* are more closely related to clams than insects, but their feeding damage is similar. With their rasping tongues they macerate plant tissue and then suck it in. Slugs and snails prefer moist conditions, and slugs especially hide under rocks, boards, or other cover on the ground.

Mites (Figure 114) damage plants by piercing the epidermis and sucking out the sap with their sharp mouthparts. The damage resembles that of lace bugs. Lace bugs, however, leave numerous specks of excrement on the lower surface of the leaves. No visible excrement is left by mites.

Sowbugs and *pillbugs* are not really insects, but are more closely related to crayfish and lobsters. These small crustaceans feed on decaying organic matter, but will occasionally feed on living plants. Sowbugs and pillbugs prefer a moist environment and are commonly found under rocks, leaf litter, and mulches.

Millipedes are similar to sowbugs in their habits. Usually scavengers, they will occasionally feed on living plants. Millipedes prefer a moist habitat, but will migrate after heavy rains. Homeowners often become alarmed at large numbers of millipedes "worming" their way into basements and garages. The housewife can vacuum or sweep them up and dispose of them easily.

114. Spider mites, about the size of a period on this page (Courtesy North Carolina Agricultural Extension Service)

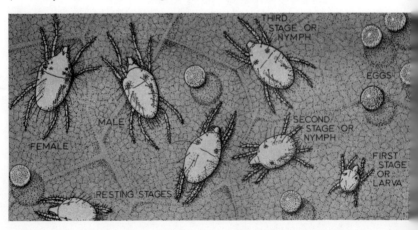

RECOMMENDED REFERENCES

Department of Pathology, *Nematode Control in Woody Ornamentals.* Plant Pathology Information Note 63, North Carolina State University, Raleigh, N.C. 27607, May 1970.

North Carolina Agricultural Extension Service, *Bagworms and Their Control.* Folder 147, North Carolina State University, Raleigh, N.C. 27607, May 1971.

————, *The Balsam Woolly Aphid.* Extension Folder No. 258, North Carolina State University, Raleigh, N.C. 27607, March 1967.

————, *Control of Aphids on Ornamentals.* Extension Folder 176, North Carolina State University, Raleigh, N.C. 27607, April 1971.

————, *Flower, Shrub, and Lawn Pests.* Insect Note No. 2, North Carolina State University, Raleigh, N.C. 27607, May 7, 1971.

————, *Galls.* Insect Note No. 5, North Carolina State University, Raleigh, N.C. 27607, May 17, 1972.

————, *Lace Bugs and Their Control.* Folder 177, North Carolina State University, Raleigh, N.C. 27607, May 1971.

————, *Leaf Feeding Insects on Trees and Shrubs.* Insect Note No. 7, North Carolina State University, Raleigh, N.C. 27607, July 5, 1972.

————, *Maple Gall Insects.* Insect Note 4, North Carolina State University, Raleigh, N.C. 27607, May 16, 1972.

————, *Millipedes and Centipedes and Their Control.* Extension Folder 252, North Carolina State University, Raleigh, N.C. 27607, August 1967.

————, *Mimosa Webworm and Its Control.* Folder 175, North Carolina State University, Raleigh, N.C. 27607, May 1971.

————, *Oak Leaf Blotchminers.* Insect Note No. 3, North Carolina State University, Raleigh, N.C. 27607, May 16, 1972.

————, *Scale Insects and Their Control.* Extension Folder No. 166, North Carolina State University, Raleigh, N.C. 27607, August 1966.

————, *Sod Webworms and Their Control in Lawns.* Insect Note No. 8, North Carolina State University, Raleigh, N.C. 27607, June 2, 1972.

————, *Spider Mite Control on Ornamentals.* Folder 164, North Carolina State University, Raleigh, N.C. 27607, May 1971.

U. S. Department of Agriculture, *Combatting the Eastern Tent Caterpillar.* Home and Garden Bulletin No. 178, Washington, D.C. 20250, October 1970.

————, *Gypsy Moth; A Major Pest of Trees.* PA-1006, Washington, D.C. 20250, May 1972.

————, *The Narcissus Bulb Fly; How to Prevent Its Damage in Home Gardens.* Leaflet No. 444, Washington, D.C. 20250, February 1969.

————, *Periodical Cicadas—"17 Year Locusts."* Leaflet No. 540, Washington, D.C. 20250, June 1971.

University of Minnesota, *Control of Scale Insects on Trees and Shrubs.* Entomology Fact Sheet No. 34, St. Paul, Minnesota, 1970.

————, *Controlling Insect Pests of Shade and Ornamental Trees.* Entomology Fact Sheet No. 28, St. Paul, Minnesota, 1970.

General Bibliography

Clemson University Extension Service, *Care of Ornamental Plants.* Circular 430, Clemson University, Clemson, S.C. 29631, May 1970.

———, *Landscape Planning for South Carolina Homes.* Circular 526, Clemson University, Clemson, S.C. 29631, November 1971.

North Carolina Agricultural Extension Service, *Landscaping Your Living Space.* Extension Circular No. 534, North Carolina State University, Raleigh, N.C. 27607, October 1971.

———, *Ph Preference of the Common Flowers, Trees, Shrubs.* Horticultural Information Leaflet No. 513, North Carolina State University, Raleigh, N.C. 27607, January 1967.

———, *Space Sculpturing with Trees and Shrubs.* Folder No. 291, North Carolina State University, Raleigh, N.C. 27607, June 1971.

Radford, A. E., Ahles, H. E., and C. R. Bell. *Atlas of the Vascular Flora of the Carolinas.* Technical Bulletin No. 165, Department of Botany, University of North Carolina, Chapel Hill, N.C., March 1965.

U. S. Department of Agriculture, *Gardening on the Contour.* Home and Garden Bulletin No. 179, Washington, D.C. 20250, June 1970.

———, *Growing Ornamentals in Urban Gardens.* Home and Garden Bulletin No. 188, Washington, D.C. 20250, May 1971.

———, *Home Planting by Design.* Home and Garden Bulletin No. 164, Washington, D.C. 20250, March 1969.

———, *The Yearbook of Agriculture.* Washington, D.C. 20250, 1972.

Usher, George. *A Dictionary of Botany.* Constable and Company, Ltd., London, 1966.

INDEX